WHEN LEGAL ORDERS COLLIDE:
THE ROLE OF COURTS

SABINO CASSESE

WHEN LEGAL ORDERS COLLIDE: THE ROLE OF COURTS

GLOBAL LAW PRESS
EDITORIAL DERECHO GLOBAL

SEVILLA · 2010

The publication of this book has been funded
by the Research Project DER2008-03366,
granted by the Spanish Ministerio de Ciencia e Innovación

© 2010: Editorial Derecho Global–Global Law Press
C/ Virgen de Luján, 19. 2° B
41011-Sevilla
info@globallawpress.org
www.globallawpress.org

Design: Los Papeles del Sitio

ISBN: 978-84-936349-2-6
DL: S-985-2010

(Printed in Spain)

CONTENTS

CHAPTER I

WHO HOLDS TOGETHER
THE LEGAL ORDERS OF THE WORLD?

INDEX

I. INTRODUCTION

S TATE sovereignty is becoming diluted. Public power is being rearticulated in pluralistic and polycentric forms. National legal orders must confront problems that are beyond their capacity to resolve alone. And onto these legal orders are superimposed a number of others, on many different levels.

This pluralism requires an order: to fill in the gaps, reduce fragmentation and induce cooperation between the different systems; to establish hierarchies of values and principles; and to introduce rules on the recognition, validity and effectiveness of norms.

In the absence of a superior legal order that imposes order among the "inferior" ones,[1] each must find within itself the instruments for cooperation with the others. And within each, it is only governments and parliaments that have responsibility for foreign policy. Yet there exist neither governments nor parliaments beyond the State; at the same time, within States, "foreign policy" has become too complex to be managed by governments alone.

---

[1] This is one of the elements studied in the numerous analyses of the "fragmentation of international law" – a theme on which there is already an abundant literature. Amongst recent examples, see Andreas Fischer-Lescano & Gunther Teubner, *Regime-Collisions: The Vain Search for Legal Unity in the Fragmentation of Global Law*, 25 MICH. J. INT'L L. 999 (2004); International Law Commission, *Conclusions of the Work of the Study Group on the Fragmentation of International Law: Difficulties Arising From the Diversification and Expansion of International Law*, (United Nations, 2006); Eyal Benvenisti & George W. Downs, *The Empire's New Clothes: Political Economy and the Fragmentation of International Law*, 60 STAN. L. REV. 595 (2007).

Judicial bodies are, however, also present in the legal space beyond the State: indeed, more than one hundred of these are full and genuine courts, to which one should also add the numerous quasi-judicial bodies and other forms of adversarial proceedings that are now present, under various different guises, in many of the roughly two thousand global regulatory regimes currently in existence.

Courts and quasi-judicial bodies, moreover, operate on a case-by-case basis. They are, therefore, able to make progressive adjustments to the law they apply, using strategies that either alternate between or blend activism and deference, law-creation and "self-restraint," dynamism and tolerance, rigidity and flexibility.

For this reason, courts are assuming an important role in the definition of the relations between different legal orders. There is much talk nowadays of "judicial dialogue" or "judicial conversation," of "inter-judicial coordination" and a "community of judges."[2]

II. FRAMING THE PROBLEM

According to the traditional criterion of the dualism between internal and external legal orders, the power to take "external" action (that is, the power within States to take foreign policy decisions) is vested in the government. Parliament supervises the exercise of this

---

[2] *See generally* Sabino Cassese, *La funzione costituzionale dei giudici non statali. Dallo spazio giuridico globale all'ordine giuridico globale*, RIVISTA TRIMESTRALE DI DIRITTO PUBBLICO 609 (2007) (which includes a number of further references on this issue). More recently still, see Eyal Benvenisti & George W. Downs, *National Checks that Balance Global Institutions: Judicial Review of International Organizations*, paper for Hauser Globalization Colloquium Fall 2008: Global Governance and Legal Theory, NYU Law School, September 24, 2008; Benedict Kingsbury, *Weighing Global Regulatory Rules and Decisions in National Courts*, ACTA JURIDICA 90 (2009); Andrea Hamann & Hélène Ruiz Fabri, *Transnational Networks and Constitutionalism*, 6 INT'L J. CONST. L. 496 (2008).

power and the administration executes it, although not in its own name, but only as the agent of the government. The judicial system, however, is absent (unless the internal legal order has "imported" or recognized certain external norms.) In this manner, the paradigm of the "State-as-a-unit" is maintained.

This structure is confronted – both in positive law and in conceptual terms – by two difficulties. Firstly, it is capable of explaining only relations between the national and the international (or supranational) levels; not those between different global regimes, in which the key actors do not display the characteristics of States, but are rather global bodies with sectoral "governments." Secondly, it has been surpassed by the disaggregation of the State, which occurs when administrative actors and judges also begin to engage in direct, cross-border dialogue with each other.

At this point, law is slowly – very slowly – taking the place of politics in the global arena. If the initial move was from soldiers to ambassadors in the resolution of international disputes, now the move is from ambassadors to judges. Courts are "crossing borders" more and more frequently (this phenomenon can also be observed in terms of bureaucracies – so called "intergovernmentalism" – and legal theory;[3] these, however, are beyond the scope of my analysis here).

The encounter between different legal orders, which can be situated at different levels (in the sense that they can be, for example, located at the national or supranational levels), is also an encounter between different legal traditions, each with its own identity. A number of different problems stem from this. One is the issue of

---

[3] Contrary to the position that "legal thinking does not cross national boundaries easily" (RICHARD A. POSNER, HOW JUDGES THINK 368 (2008)).

"sustainable diversity,"[4] in the sense of tolerance and mutual adaptation. Another is that of the constitution of a "common core" of principles, drawn from each of the legal traditions in question; a third is that of the recognition of a minimum body of superior principles (such as *jus cogens* in international law.)

III. RELATIONS BETWEEN NATIONAL AND SUPRANATIONAL ORDERS, AND BETWEEN GLOBAL REGIMES

Two different types of relations have developed as a result of the pluralization of public power discussed above. On the one hand, there are those between national or State orders, and "superior," supranational or international ones. On the other, there are the relations between the different – and by now extremely numerous – global legal orders. Strictly speaking, a further set of relations should also be considered: those containing mixed elements of the first and second types.

As noted previously, these relations are not governed by superior principles; a cooperative effort is thus required if collisions are to be avoided. This effort must be incremental, both in order to avoid upsetting the delicate balance between coexisting legal orders, and because it is, in large part, voluntary (in the sense that it is not imposed by a superior order).

The difficulties that must be overcome with regard to the first type of relations concern coordination between non-hierarchical forms of interaction between orders, in which a principle of primacy is developed through quasi-voluntary forms of cooperation. The difficulties with regard to coordination and reciprocal adjustment

---

[4] H. Patrick Glenn, Legal Traditions of the World 331 (2000).

are equally present in the second type of relation; however, there is also the problem of how to construct, from the bottom up, a body of shared principles, rules or values capable of constituting a general "corpus" common to the different sectoral regimes. In both cases, there is the additional difficulty of maintaining control over or limiting the impact of the diverse possibilities – in terms of choice of law and of choice of forum – that are the consequences of pluralization. In essence, the challenge is to ensure that the individual planets and the universe as a whole can co-exist.[5]

IV. LEGAL ORDERS AND COURTS

An examination of the problems outlined above must – as already noted – proceed in two directions at once: it must focus both on the relations between domestic and extra-State legal orders, and those between global regulatory regimes.

Two main themes alternate in the second of these spheres: the fragmentation of legal orders ("self-contained global regimes"), and the proliferation of heterarchically-organized international courts ("a Babel of judicial voices").[6] A number of reciprocal influences between these two phenomena have been identified, albeit pulling in different directions.

---

[5] Bruno Simma, *Ein endlose Geschichte? Artikel 36 der Wiener Konsularkonvention in Todesstrafenfällen vor dem IGH und amerikanishen Gerichten*, in VÖLKERRECHT ALS WERTORDNUNG: FESTSCHRIFT FÜR CHRISTIAN TOMUSCHAT/ COMMON VALUES IN INTERNATIONAL LAW: ESSAYS IN HONOUR OF CHRISTIAN TOMUSCHAT 423 (Pierre-Marie Dupuy et al eds., 2006).

[6] Rosalyn Higgins, *A Babel of Judicial Voices? Ruminations from the Bench*, 55 INT'L & COMP. L.Q. 791 (2006). On the proliferation of courts, see the research conducted within the "Project on International Courts and Tribunal" (www.pict-pcti.org).

Some, for example, view fragmentation as a product of the proliferation of international courts.[7] In particular, the claim made is that the growth in the number of international tribunals has gone hand in hand with the development of divergent and contrasting lines of jurisprudence. For this reason, it is argued, the general competence to determine issues of customary international law or to interpret international treaties should be vested only, or at least principally, in the International Court of Justice. In this way, the principle of the unity of the law would be protected.

According to others, however, the multiplication of tribunals represents a step forward for international law: if the basic activity of courts is to "gather, interpret and develop the law,"[8] then the increase in the number of supranational judges should simply extend and strengthen that function. Moreover, the "specialization" of different judicial fora should serve to limit the potential for overlapping competences and judgments. In this sense, the proliferation of tribunals can be considered as one means of overcoming the fragmentation of sectoral legal orders and creating a connective tissue of common principles between them.

The works by Yuval Shany on these issues, on *Regulating Jurisdictional Relations Between National and International Courts* and *Competing Jurisdictions of International Courts and Tribunals*,[9] examine

---

[7] Shigeru Oda, *Dispute Settlement Prospects in the Law of the Sea*, 44 INT'L & COMP. L.Q. 863 (1995). See, in particular, his claim that "[t]he rule of law based upon the uniform development of jurisprudence will be best secured by strengthening the role of the International Court of Justice, not by dispersing the judicial function of dispute settlement in the international community among various scattered organs. The Convention is so misguided as to deprive the Court of its role as the sole organ for the judicial settlement of ocean disputes by setting up a new judicial institution, the ITLOS, in parallel with the long-established Court" (*id.* at 864).

[8] TULLIO TREVES, LE CONTROVERSIE INTERNAZIONALI. NUOVE TENDENZE, NUOVI TRIBUNALI 59-67 (1999).

[9] YUVAL SHANY, THE COMPETING JURISDICTIONS OF INTERNATIONAL COURTS AND TRIBUNALS (2003); YUVAL SHANY, REGULATING JURISDICTIONAL RELATIONS BETWEEN NATIONAL AND INTERNATIONAL COURTS (2007).

both types of "judicial interaction" from the perspective of overlapping or conflicting jurisdictions. It is, however, also interesting to consider the same argument from a different perspective: that of the contribution of judges to the establishment of either an order, or a "connective tissue," between two regimes. In this case, more emphasis is placed on substantive rather than procedural aspects.[10] The concern here, then, is not with regulating the activity of judges, but rather with ascertaining whether they are succeeding in regulating the pluralization of public power and in contributing to the development of a common legal order. From this standpoint, courts are to be considered not in their passive role, to which issues relating to the limitation and exercise of jurisdiction are central, but rather in their active role, as creators of an order quite different from that dominated by pluralization.

It is clear that the two aspects outlined above are closely related in a number of ways. For example, constitutional courts within the EU have been keen to safeguard their own role in defining the relations between the Community legal order and the internal orders of Member States.

V. THE INTEGRATIVE ROLE OF JUDGES: HOW IS IT PERFORMED AND WITH WHAT RESULTS?

My basic hypothesis in this paper is, therefore, that courts fulfill an important role in removing from isolation the various different legal orders existing at various different levels. It is thus important to establish how this happens and with what results; inquire as to why, for example, the Belgian, Austrian and Czech Constitutional

---

[10] But – as we will see – the emphasis is not primarily on those substantive aspects related to the rights-protecting role of judges, such as ensuring respect for the "due process of law."

Courts make direct use of preliminary references to the European Court of Justice, while those of Germany, France and Italy do not; or how national laws, and those of other global regimes, are treated by international commercial tribunals or the International Tribunal for the Law of the Sea.

An essential component of this integrative role of courts is composed of a number of "doctrines" that enable cooperation, each acting as a "clutch" for connecting or disconnecting legal systems, as "glue" that holds them together or as a rhetorical device that enables judges to more readily exercise restraint.[11]

These doctrines can be listed as follows:

a. Counter-limits (where a "superior" law is accepted by an "inferior" legal order, on the condition that the former respects the fundamental principles of the latter);

b. Margin of appreciation (where a "superior" law is imposed upon "inferior" legal orders, but leaves a certain margin of freedom to the latter);

c. The distinction between supremacy and primacy (where a "superior" law applies within "inferior" legal orders not as the result of its hierarchical superiority, but rather on the basis of the spheres of competence of the two orders);

d. Atypical or infra-constitutional sources; "interposed rules" (where a "superior" law is imposed upon the ordinary legislation of the "inferior" legal order, but not upon its constitutional laws);

e. Direct effect and "interpretation in conformity" (where a "superior" law, although not directly addressed to private actors, obliges the

---

[11] The issue of the necessary interconnections between different legal orders beyond the State has been examined in two recent studies. *See* Neil Walker, *Beyond Boundary Disputes and Basic Grids: Mapping the Global Disorder of Normative Orders*, 6 INT'L J. CONST. L. 373 (2008); Michel Rosenfeld, *Rethinking Constitutional Ordering in an Era of Legal and Ideological Pluralism*, 6 INT'L J. CONST. L. 415 (2008).

authorities of the "inferior" legal order to apply their norms in conformity with the "superior" law);

f. "Judicial comity," referrals or "deference" among regulatory regimes (where different extra-State legal orders are treated as integrated or as bound by obligations of cooperation);

g. Equivalent protection (where one legal order recognizes the validity of another on the condition that the latter guarantees a level of protection of fundamental rights comparable to that furnished by the former);

h. Division of functions (where one legal order makes room for another in relation to a particular function, where the principal role of the latter is to fulfill that function);

i. Subsidiarity (where a legal order abstains from intervening in a particular matter over which another legal order, less removed from the interests at stake, has jurisdiction).

These issues will be examined in the following order. The first section will consider a number of examples of convergence and divergence of interests between national and supra-State legal orders, and between global legal orders. The second will examine two disputes in which judicial or quasi-judicial bodies were called upon to resolve conflicts between different legal orders, located at various different levels. The third and largest section will review a number of key examples, chosen from among the many available today, in which judicial or quasi-judicial bodies define the modalities of connection between different legal orders, whether situated on the same or on different levels. The final section will conclude by drawing together the various threads of the analysis.

My inquiry here will depart from an examination of concrete cases. In the area of interest to us here, approximate and general ideas abound; and these often lead to similarly general and abstract conclusions. These include, for example, the claims that it is always States that, in the final instance, resolve conflicts and establish relations with other legal orders; that globalization is primarily an economic phenomenon, which, in the field of law and institutions, is dependent upon the consent of the parties; or that non-State legal orders are destined to remain mere isolated monads until the constitution of a superior, global order. The analysis that follows seeks to demonstrate that theory, if it is to be capable of grasping new phenomena, cannot simply content itself with these *idées reçues*. It must instead engage in a detailed collection and examination of the basic data in order to then ascertain their importance and their potential to modify our traditional paradigms.

CHAPTER II

CONVERGENCE AND DIVERGENCE OF INTERESTS IN THE GLOBAL ARENA

INDEX

I. INTRODUCTION

T HE global arena is characterized by the absence of a unitary legal order and of a hierarchy of norms, by the presence of a great many non-binding norms (standards and "soft law"), and by competition or conflict between legal orders; moreover, it lacks a requirement of obedience (in place of which are mechanisms of compliance). In such a context, how can different legal orders coexist?

I will seek to respond to this question firstly by examining six examples,[12] which will enable us to draw some conclusions regarding the structure of interests in the global arena, before going on to illustrate the ways in which judges weave the web of relations between the different legal orders. The first part of the investigation is, therefore, more sociological in character; the second, more legal.

---

[12] The six examples are 1) the agreements, concluded on 5 May 2008, between the Italian and Chinese Governments, and between Enel and the Chinese group "Wuhan Iron & Steel Corp.," within the framework of the Kyoto Protocol's Clean Development Mechanism; 2) the proposal of the UN Special Representative on Human Rights, presented to the Human Rights Council, on the need to recognize and to regulate the responsibility of corporations to respect human rights; 3) the Communication from the European Commission of the 20th of March 2008, proposing a number of measures intended to respond to the emergence of so-called "agriflation;" 4) the agreement of September 2007 between the UN and the State of Guatemala, establishing the International Commission Against Impunity in Guatemala (ICAIG); 5) the creation of the new "wikileaks.org" website, and the emergence of "whistleblowers" at the global level; and 6) the recent proposal by the French Minister for Foreign Affairs, Bernard Kouchner, regarding the application of the "responsibility to protect" principle in the context of natural disasters.

II. THE ENVIRONMENTAL MEMORANDUM OF UNDER-STANDING BETWEEN THE ITALIAN AND CHINESE GOVERNMENTS

On the 5th of May 2008, two agreements were signed in Beijing: the first, a Memorandum of Understanding between the Governments of Italy and China; the second, a contract between Enel, Italy's largest power company, and the Wuhan Iron & Steel Corporation, the second largest iron and steel company in China.[13] On the basis of these agreements, Enel, together with the Italian Government, is to provide consultancy services in order to promote and encourage the spread within China of technologies enabling a cleaner use of carbon (so-called "clean coal technologies"). In exchange, Enel acquired from the Chinese Government allowances for the emission of carbon dioxide (so-called "green certificates" or certified emission reductions). The agreements are intended to help reduce the intake of CO_2 into the atmosphere, in conformity with the Kyoto Protocol.[14]

The carbon dioxide emission allowances (with a total value of one hundred and fifty million euro), so-called "carbon credits" (derived from projects for improving the energy efficiency of the Chinese company),[15] still required, however, the approval of the UN and of the Chinese Government before they could be traded.

---

[13] The Wuhan Iron & Steel Corp. is listed on the Shanghai Stock Exchange, produces nine million tons of iron and steel every year, and is considered the second largest Chinese iron and steel group in terms of capitalization.

[14] More precisely, the agreement consists in a Memorandum of Understanding signed by Enel, the Minister for Science and Technology of the People's Republic of China, and the Italian Minister for the Environment, and falls within the ambit of the "Sino-Italian Cooperation Program for Environmental Protection," initiated in 2001 with the objective of identifying project opportunities intended to promote sustainable development in China. Moreover, the agreement also fits within the framework of the activities begun by ENEL and the Minister for the Environment, beginning in 2004, with the aim of reducing greenhouse gas emissions in China. To programs such as these can further be added the preparation of a memorandum of understanding between the Italian and Chinese Governments on the development of "eco-sustainable" cities in certain areas of China.

[15] In particular, the contract was for the acquisition by Enel of allowances relating to five projects in energy efficiency aimed at reducing CO_2 emissions totaling 11.45 million metric tons from 2008 to 2012.

From this exchange, the Chinese Government obtained benefits in terms of limiting the environmental impact of its electrical energy production activities through the reduction by more than a third of the carbon dioxide emissions produced for every megawatt generated; the Italian company, for its part, was able to respect CO_2 emission targets by using the allowances acquired for the construction of coal-fired power stations at Civitavecchia and at Porto Tolle.

These agreements fall within the framework of the Clean Development Mechanism, one of the three mechanisms established by the Kyoto Protocol.[16] This system, defined as one of "mutual benefit," enables exchanges that aim at once to increase environmental protection and to develop the market. China can save billions of tons of carbon dioxide each year by applying the technologies sold by Enel; at the same time, Enel is able, thanks to its acquisition of emission allowances, to increase the number of its own plants while respecting the limits laid down by the Kyoto Protocol, remaining in compliance with sustainable development programs.[17]

This example involves two national legal orders (those of Italy and China), operating on a global level on the basis of an extra-State legal system (established by the Kyoto Protocol). Also involved are two important collective interests, relating to the production

---

[16] The other two mechanisms are those of Joint Implementation and Emissions Trading. The Clean Development Mechanism is regulated by Article 12 of the Kyoto Protocol and applies to the relations between those countries, such as Italy, subject to limits on their emissions (these limits are contained in Annex B of the Protocol), and those not subject to any limits, such as China. The Mechanism provides for the conclusion of agreements between these two categories of countries. The objects of these agreements are projects financed by developed countries in countries not subject to limits in order to increase non-polluting production and reduce emissions in those countries. In exchange, the financing countries obtain "credits" for the reduction of emissions (this is the so-called "credit trading"). On this issue, see Jessica F. Green, *Delegation to Private Actors: A Study of the Clean Development Mechanism*, IILJ Emerging Scholars Papers, ESP 5[2007]. *More generally, see* SABINO CASSESE, LA CRISI DELLO STATO 9-14 (2002).

[17] It is worth noting that Enel has already finalized more than 60 projects for the abatement of greenhouse gas emissions in order to invest in less efficient markets, thus achieving – through the same economic effort - greater environmental benefits, in compliance with the Kyoto Protocol.

of electricity and environmental protection respectively, over and above the commercial interests in play. Ultimately, the interests of the two orders converge.

III. THE UNITED NATIONS PROPOSAL ON CORPORATE RESPONSIBILITY FOR HUMAN RIGHTS

On the 3rd of June 2008, the United Nations Special Representative on Human Rights presented to the UN Human Rights Council a proposal on corporate responsibility to respect human rights.[18] Its purpose, set out in the first paragraph of the proposal, is to ensure "more effective protection to individuals and communities against corporate-related human rights harm." This objective is to be pursued through a "principles-based conceptual and policy framework" set out in the proposal itself. In particular, paragraph 55 affirms the principle that corporations must respect human rights independently of the analogous duties of States.[19] In other words, there is no need to distinguish between "'primary' State and 'secondary' corporate obligations." This would thus establish the direct and primary responsibility of corporations, independently of any recognition of the responsibility of their home States. Corporations would have to insert the respect for human rights into their own codes of conduct and would be eligible to receive financial support

---

[18] Report of the Special Representative of the Secretary General on the issue of human rights and transnational corporation and other business enterprises, *Promotion and protection of all human rights, civil, political, economic, social and cultural rights, including the right to development*, A/HRC/8/5, 7 April 2008. *See also* John H. Knox, *Horizontal Human Rights Law*, 102 AM. J. INT'L L. 1 (2008).

[19] Paragraph 55 reads as follows: "The corporate responsibility to respect exists independently of States' duties. Therefore, there is no need for the slippery distinction between 'primary' State and 'secondary' corporate obligations – which in any event would invite endless strategic gaming on the ground about who is responsible for what. Furthermore, because the responsibility to respect is a baseline expectation, a company cannot compensate for human rights harm by performing good deeds elsewhere. Finally, 'doing no harm' is not merely a passive responsibility for firms but may entail positive steps – for example, a workplace anti-discrimination policy might require the company to adopt specific recruitment and training programmes."

from States for their export activities, above all in conflict zones, only if they offer guarantees that these rights will be respected.[20]

This proposal has already given rise to a number of issues. For example, Coca-Cola and its Managing Director, Neville Isdell (himself a member of many human rights organizations),[21] were criticized for their sponsorship of the Olympic Games in Beijing. The Chinese Government had been accused of atrocities in Tibet and of tolerating and even defending grave violations of human rights in Myanmar and in Darfur, to the extent that the Beijing Games came to be defined in public opinion as the "genocide Olympics."[22] A number of supranational associations working in the field of human rights, such as the NGO Human Rights Watch, denounced the complicity in human rights abuses and the conspiracy of silence of the businesses that finance the Olympic Games, among which is Coca-Cola. As had happened in South Africa during the struggle against apartheid,[23] the belief was that a "reaction" by the corporations could contribute to improving the protection of human rights in China.

This example involved one national legal order (China) and two global ones (the International Olympic Committee and the UN). Two global regulatory systems – for human rights and for sport – came into conflict. In the end, both convergence and divergence can be observed between the different interests in play.

---

[20] On this point, see the interesting report published on the 16th of September 2008 by the International Commission of Jurists, which had established, in September 2006, an Expert Legal Panel on Corporate Complicity in International Crimes monitoring the conduct of corporations with respect to human rights. The report is available at www.business-humanrights.org/Updates/Archive/ICJPaneloncomplicity.

[21] More specifically, the Managing Director of Coca-Cola is a member of the UN Global Compact and of the Business Leaders Initiative on Human Rights; moreover, under his management, Coca-Cola is financing numerous projects in Darfur aimed at supporting the local population and protecting human rights.

[22] See, on this point, the article *Beyond the "genocide Olympics,"* THE ECONOMIST, 24 April 2008.

[23] With reference to the actions taken by a number of multinational corporations against apartheid in South Africa.

IV. COMMUNITY AGRICULTURAL POLICY AND "AGRI-FLATION"

During the past six years, the prices of wheat, corn, rice and soya have risen in every State in the world.[24] This global phenomenon has been termed "agriflation."[25] The increase in prices is due to a number of different causes: the use of certain food products in the production of biofuels,[26] part of the effort to develop alternative forms of energy; the drop in supply, due, alongside natural disasters, to the application of the Community scheme for reducing the arable land under production[27] (a program intended to support farmers, who were thus able at certain points in the past, when food prices were very low and supply was greater than demand, to avoid excess production and cope with costs); the improvement in living conditions in certain large countries, such as India and China, which has led to a strong increase in the demand for meat at the global level (the growth in consumption of meat also involves the use of some products, such as wheat and corn, for the sustenance of livestock); and increases in transportation and freight costs.

---

[24] It is calculated that between 2007 and 2008 the average growth in food prices has been 50%, with peaks of 70% for rice (the price of which has risen in 2008 in particular), of almost 90% for soya and 130% for wheat (the price of which rose particularly in 2007). The World Bank has predicted that prices will remain high for all of 2008 and 2009, after which they will start to fall in successive years – although it also predicts that in 2015 prices will nevertheless remain higher than they were in 2004.

[25] The term "agriflation" is intended to mean the increase in food prices, which was seen in 2007 in particular. The term was coined by Merrill Lynch, a major investment bank based in New York that was an early casualty of the financial crisis.

[26] Biofuels are propellants indirectly obtained from biomass: wheat, corn, sugar beet, sugar cane, etc. The following are considered to be biofuels: bioethanol, biodiesel, bi-omethanol, biodimethylether, synthetic hydrocarbons, biohydrogen, and vegetable oils. For more information, see http://en.wikipedia.org/wiki/Biofuel.

[27] The relevant law is contained in Council Regulation (EC) No. 1782/2003 of 29 September 2003 "establishing common rules for direct support schemes under the common agricultural policy and establishing certain support schemes for farmers and amending Regulations (EEC) No. 2019/93, (EC) No. 1452/2001, (EC) No. 1453/2001, (EC) No. 1454/2001, (EC) No. 1868/94, (EC) No. 1251/1999, (EC) No. 1254/1999, (EC) No. 1673/2000, (EEC) No. 2358/71 and (EC) No. 2529/2001."

The consequences of "agriflation" include increases in the cost of living, above all in countries that import basic foodstuffs, and a growth in levels of starvation in the world.

Many extra-State organizations have reacted to this situation. The UN Special Rapporteur on the Right to Food raised the alarm, highlighting a "food crisis," which would lead to the "silent massacre" of many of the world's vulnerable.[28] The World Bank has invited the international community to respond to the emergency: the high price of rice risks pushing a hundred million people below the poverty line.[29]

In 2007, the Council of the European Community suspended for 2008 the obligation on farmers in the EU Member States to remove from production 10% of their arable land (the "set aside requirement"),[30] in derogation from Regulation EC No. 1782/2003.[31] In May 2008, the European Commission proposed to the Council and to the European Parliament a series of measures intended both to mitigate the effects of the price increases in the short- to medium-term (and to increase the supply of basic foodstuffs in the long-term), as well as to lessen the effects of the crisis at the international level.[32] In July

---

[28] This expression is taken from an article by Danilo Taino, *L'inviato Onu: "La crisi del cibo è uno sterminio silenzioso*," IL CORRIERE DELLA SERA, 21 April 2008.

[29] To these can also be added interventions by the International Monetary Fund (IMF) and the Food and Agriculture Organization (FAO).

[30] In Italy, this amounted to around 250,000 hectares of arable land.

[31] See Council Regulation (EC) No. 1107/2007 of 26 September 2007 "derogating from Regulation (EC) No. 1782/2003 establishing common rules for direct support schemes under the common agricultural policy and establishing certain support schemes for farmers, as regards set-aside for the year 2008."

[32] See the Communication from the Commission to the European Parliament, the Council, the European Economic and Social Committee and the Committee of the Regions, "Tackling the challenge of rising food prices: Directions for EU action", Brussels, 20 May 2008, COM(2008) 321. The measures proposed by way of an immediate response to the emergency were adjusting the common agricultural policy; acting for the most deprived persons; investigating the functioning of the food supply chain; avoiding measures with distortionary effects; and analyzing speculative investments. The long-term measures mainly concerned the production of biofuels and GMOs. Lastly, concerning the measures for responding to the crisis at the international level, bringing the Doha Round of negotiations to an early conclusion and the strengthening of Community action in the field of

2008, the Commission proposed a special financing system, including a fund of one billion euro to assist farmers in developing countries.[33]

Therefore, this example implicates legal orders located at three different levels: national, supranational (the European Community) and global (the UN, the World Bank, the IMF, and the FAO). A number of collective interests are also involved, relating to the protection of the environment, to energy development, and to the protection of human life. Ultimately, a singular paradox emerges, in which the improvements in quality of life and the development of stronger environmental protections produce, indirectly, a deterioration in the conditions of subsistence of a part of the world's population.

V. THE SECURITY PROBLEM IN GUATEMALA

In February 2008, twelve bus drivers were assassinated in Guatemala.[34] Guatemala has been a democratic State since 1985, and its civil war has now been over for some time; nevertheless, its civil and democratic institutions remain unable to assert themselves even today. Guatemala has one of the highest rates of violence of any State in the world (forty-three murders for every hundred thousand inhabitants, annually). Alongside these extremely high rates of criminality sit similarly high rates of impunity; indeed, only 2% of murders committed ever become the object of judicial proceedings.

---

human rights were proposed. The proposal was accepted by the European Council in the document containing the conclusions of the President of the EU Council of 20 June 2008 (CONCL 2, 11018/08).

[33] Notification of the proposal is available on the "Press Release Rapid" section of the website of the European Union: (http://europa.eu/rapid/pressReleasesAction.do?reference=IP/08/1186&format=HTML&aged=0&language=IT&guiLanguage=en). Moreover, in the context of the scheme for controlling the price of cereals, Regulation (EC) No. 1039/2008 of 22 October 2008 "reintroducing customs duties on imports of certain cereals for the 2008/09 marketing year" was adopted.

[34] This was reported in *A test of will:Guatemala*, THE ECONOMIST, 22 March 2008.

In order to stem the rising crime rate and to resolve the serious problem of the inefficiency of the Guatemalan judicial administration, The UN concluded with the State of Guatemala an agreement for the establishment of an extra-State body charged with intervening in the administration of justice in Guatemala in order to promote prosecutions.[35] In May of 2007, the Guatemalan Constitutional Court declared that the agreement was in conformity with the Constitution, rejecting, however, the possibility that the new body could itself make accusations or engage in the actual prosecution of crime.[36] The Constitutional Court had already ruled out the original idea, promoted in particular by human rights organizations, of constituting an independent supranational court for the country with investigative functions in the field of organized crime, on the grounds that this would violate Guatemalan national sovereignty. In August 2007, the Guatemalan Parliament approved the agreement; in September of the same year, the International Commission Against Impunity in Guatemala (ICAIG) was established.

The Commission has investigative powers and promotes the prosecution of guilty parties before the national courts. As established in the constitutive agreement (Art. 1(1)(a)), the international community is, through this institution, providing assistance to the Guatemalan Government. The agreement grants to the Commission complete functional independence, and the power to collect, evaluate and classify all relevant information on offences, to promote the criminal prosecution of suspects, to provide technical assistance, and to communicate to the competent authorities the names of public officials who are not fulfilling their duties.[37]

This example brings together a national legal order (Guatemala) and a global one (the UN). Respect for the rule of law is in both the

---

[35] A complete account of the facts of this situation and an up-to-date list of relevant documents is available at www.humanrightsfirst.org/defenders/hrd_guatemala/hrd_cicig.asp.

[36] The text of the decision is available at www.humanrightsfirst.info/pdf/07511-hrd-cicig-press-release-sp.pdf.

[37] The functions and powers of the Commission are specifically regulated by Articles 2 and 3 of the agreement, respectively. The text of the agreement is available at www.humanrightsfirst.info/pdf/061215-hrd-digned-english-agreement-cicig.pdf.

national and the global interest; there is, therefore, full convergence between the interests involved.

VI. "THE GOLDEN AGE OF CYBERACTIVISM"

In December 2006, a new section of the "Wikipedia" website, named "wikileaks" was created by authors initially unknown.[38] It is an organization whose basic role is to "leak" the misdeeds of Governments to the whole world, by publishing secret documents and information.[39] The materials published on the site are provided by "whistleblowers" (informers),[40] who work for public institutions, private companies, government agencies, or international organizations, and whose identity remains secret thanks to the sophisticated cryptographic technology used within the site and the fact that the IP addresses of contributors are hidden. In this sense, something of a legal limbo in cyberspace has been created. The website uses internet service providers located in Sweden and in Belgium, and thus the organization enjoys the higher levels of protection provided for within those legal orders.

The organization appeals to the "citizens of the net" (so-called "netizens" or "cybercitizens"),[41] and has become very successful in encouraging people to report facts and documents of collective interest. It has been calculated that, since 2006, more than one million documents have been published on the website, amongst which, for example, were the training manual for the prison guards at Guantanamo and a document relating to the costs incurred by the UK Government in its bailout of the Northern Rock bank.

---

[38] See www.wikileaks.org.

[39] For a historical account of the organization and its activities, see http://en.wikipedia.org/wiki/Wikileaks.

[40] A "whistle blower" is defined as "an employee, former employee, or member of an organization, especially a business or government agency, who reports misconduct to people or entities that have the power and presumed willingness to take corrective action" (definition from http://en.wikipedia.org/wiki/Whistleblower).

[41] A "netizen" is defined as "a person actively involved in online communities" (definition from http://en.wikipedia.org/wiki/Netizen).

The activity of this website was discovered in January 2007, when the editor of *Secrecy News*, a publication that has revealed numerous government and military secrets, was invited to take part in the Advisory Board[42] of the organization. By February 2008, the Federal Court of San Francisco had condemned the site;[43] yet still today numerous materials are published on Wikileaks in violation of copyright.[44]

The development of this "dangerous" online community has concerned many Governments, in particular those of China, Turkey and the Arab countries, which have blocked the use of the domain or, in some cases, filtered its content. According to some,[45] the reactions of these Governments may bring an end to the so-called "golden age of cyberactivism."

In this controversy, we have national legal orders (those of the US, China, Turkey, the Arab countries) and a global order (that

---

[42] The members of this organ are for the most part political activists, mathematicians, computer scientists, lawyers, journalists, writers, etc.

[43] The Court ordered the operator (Dynadot LCC) to disconnect the DNS, the system that creates the association between the wikileaks.org domain and the computer that physically hosts the site. The operator was also required to "immediately clear and remove all DNS hosting records for the wikileaks.org domain name and prevent the domain name from resolving to the wikileaks.org website or any other website or server other than a blank park page, until further order of this Court." Later, however, the Court in fact reversed part of this decision, ordering that the DNS be restored but that the documents that had been the object of the dispute be removed. In any event, this judgment did not completely impair the visibility of the site on the internet, which remained accessible via its numerical address.

[44] It's worth noting that the activity of wikileaks has been compared to the book *Pentagon Papers* by Daniel Ellsberg (1971), on the secrets of the Pentagon. In the United States, leaking political information through the publication of documents is a legally protected activity. *See* the case *New York Times Co. v. United States*, 403 U.S. 713 (1971). The Supreme Court established that it was possible for the New York Times and Washington Post newspapers to publish the Pentagon Papers without risk of government censure. President Nixon had claimed executive authority to force the Times to suspend publication of classified information. The question before the judges was whether the constitutional freedom of the press under the First Amendment was subordinate to a claimed Executive need to maintain the secrecy of information. The Court ruled that the First Amendment protects the newspapers' right to publish this information.

[45] *See* the article *Leaks and Lawsuits: The internet and government*, THE ECONOMIST, 8 March 2008.

relating to the internet, governed by the Internet Corporation for Assigned Names and Numbers – ICANN).[46] The interests involved are principally those pertaining to the freedom of expression and of information, and to the protection of public order. Here, these interests are in conflict.

VII. THE "RESPONSIBILITY TO PROTECT" PRINCIPLE

In a diplomatic meeting held at the UN in May 2008, the French Minister for Foreign Affairs, Bernard Kouchner, declared, in connection with the natural disasters that had occurred in the State of Myanmar, that "it would only take half an hour for the French helicopters to reach the disaster area." He proposed, in other words, the application to the case of Myanmar of the "responsibility to protect" principle.[47] However, the Governments of Myanmar and those of a number of other countries (such as Russia, China, Vietnam and South Africa) opposed the application of such a principle, refusing to accept any form of interference with State sovereignty.

Article 2(7) of the UN Charter provides that "nothing contained in the present Charter shall authorize the United Nations to intervene in matters which are essentially within the domestic jurisdiction of any state... ." Article 39 of the Charter, however, authorizes the Security Council to intervene in the case of a "threat to the peace, breach of the peace or act of aggression,"[48] both in conflicts within and between States.[49]

---

[46] The Internet Corporation for Assigned Names and Numbers (ICANN) is a Californian organization that regulates the system of domain names at the global level, carrying out the functions both of a standardizing and a governing body.

[47] This principle, developed in the realm of international politics, is based on the argument that the protection of human lives can, in extreme circumstances, justify violations of national sovereignty. *See* Carlo Focarelli, *La dottrina della "responsabilità di proteggere" e l'intervento umanitario*, 91 RIVISTA DI DIRITTO INTERNAZIONALE 317 (2008).

[48] This norm provides the foundation for the "peace mission" of the UN. See, on this point, P. PICONE, COMUNITÀ INTERNAZIONALE E OBBLIGHI "ERGA OMNES" 207-296 (2006); and, on peacekeeping activities, at 319-349.

[49] *See*, on this point, the article *The UN and humanitarian intervention: To protect sover-*

One step forward was made in 2001, when the International Commission on Intervention and State Sovereignty (ICISS)[50] proposed transforming the right of intervention into a principle of "responsibility to protect."[51] This issue was also considered within the framework of the UN Reform of 2004.[52] At the UN World Summit of 2005, the principle of responsibility to protect was recognized for the first time in cases of genocide, war crimes, ethnic cleansing and crimes against humanity.[53] In particular, paragraph 139 of the Summit Outcomes established that "[t]he international community, through the United Nations, also has the responsibility to use appropriate diplomatic, humanitarian and other peaceful means, in accordance with Chapters VI and VIII of the Charter, to help protect populations from genocide, war crimes, ethnic cleansing, and crimes against humanity."

The statement by the French Foreign Minister in the context of Myanmar would, in effect, broaden the scope of the principle to include also cases of natural disasters.[54]

---

eignty, or to protect lives?, THE ECONOMIST, 17 May 2008.

[50] The website of the Commission can be found at www.iciss-ciise.gc.ca/menu-en.asp.

[51] The text of the report is available at www.iciss-ciise.gc.ca/pdf/Commission-Report. pdf. It considers the problem of the limitations on State sovereignty, derived from the application of the responsibility to protect principle. A number of further principles, linked to that of the responsibility to protect, also feature in the report: the "responsibility to prevent," the "responsibility to react" and the "responsibility to rebuild." It also considers the problem of the bases of legitimacy of interventions undertaken in putting the principle into practice, indicating the UN Charter as the principal normative reference, and discusses the role of the UN Security Council and the possibilities for intervention available to it, both peaceful and military.

[52] *See*, in this context, the Report of the UN Secretary General, published on the section of the UN website dedicated to UN Reform (www.un-ngls.org/sg-report.htm). In paragraph 135 of the Report, in the section relating to the "Rule of Law," the Secretary General declared, in response to the report of the ICISS, his belief "that we must embrace the responsibility to protect, and, when necessary, we must act on it."

[53] The document is available at www.who.int/hiv/universalaccess2010/worldsummit. pdf.

[54] It's worth noting that the UN has created a Task Force to deal with cases of natural disaster, headed by the Under-Secretary-General for Humanitarian Affairs and Emergency Relief Coordinator, who, in July 2008, visited the sites in Myanmar worst hit by the cyclone.

This controversy involves a national legal order (that of Myanmar) and a global one (the UN). The interests in play – and in conflict – are humanitarian on one hand, and that of the State in defending its sovereignty on the other.

VIII. CONVERGENCE AND DIVERGENCE

The examples outlined above relate to eight different substantive issues: energy production; environmental protection; sports regulation; human rights; agriculture and food production; justice and public order; freedom of expression; and disaster relief. They thus concern a wide variety of typical sectors of public action that, in turn, correspond to areas in which a number of the principal problems confronting modern society and modern economics have emerged.

In these examples, numerous different legal orders meet: seven global orders, one supranational order, and six national orders. The seven global orders are the regulatory system of the Kyoto Protocol, the UN, the IOC, the FAO, the World Bank, the IMF, and ICANN. The supranational order is the European Community; and the six national orders are those of Italy, China, the US, Guatemala, Turkey, and Myanmar. Each order has one or more interests to safeguard.

Many different relations exist between the interests protected in these legal orders, of which it is now possible to set out a taxonomy. Firstly, there are global public interests that converge with either private or national interests (as in the example of the environmental Memorandum of Understanding between Italy and China). Secondly, there are global public interests that partially converge with national private interests, but conflict with national public interests (as in the controversy over the responsibility of corporations for human rights violations). Thirdly, there are global public interests that conflict with each other (as in the example of "agriflation"). Fourthly, there are cases of convergence between national public interests and global public interests (as the Guatemalan example illustrates). Lastly, there are cases in which national public interest and global public interest conflict (as in the examples of Wikileaks and Myanmar).

What are the consequences of this analysis of the convergence and divergence of interests in the global arena? In the absence of a uniform order and of pre-established relationships between the legal systems through which these interests are represented, a wide variety of different interactions and structures can be observed. There is a lack of systemic or general rules capable of regulating the ways in which relations between legal orders are both framed and balanced (such as, for example, rules of recognition, of hierarchy, of supremacy between the norms of different orders).

CHAPTER III

NEITHER SOLDIERS NOR AMBASSADORS, BUT JUDGES

INDEX

I. THE *SWORDFISH* DISPUTE

I N a world without general rules or first principles yet full of sectoral legal orders beyond those of nation-States, and without one authority hierarchically superior to the others yet rich in conflicts, how can harmony – or at least coexistence – be ensured? It is here that judges have a role to play; I now turn to an examination of this role, taking as a point of departure two controversies characterized by the involvement of multiple legal regimes, different kinds of subjects, conflicting interests, and extra-State judicial or quasi-judicial bodies interacting with each other. I will begin by setting out the main aspects of each dispute, before moving on to an analysis of the characteristics common to both.

The *Swordfish* controversy concerned a dispute between the European Community and the State of Chile.[55] Spanish boats had been fishing for swordfish in the south-eastern Pacific, in an area of the high seas adjacent to the Chilean exclusive economic zone. Chile, a country with more than four thousand kilometers of coastline, and concerned over the depletion of fish stocks in general and those of migratory species in particular, had prohibited (through two laws, in 1991 and 1999) the unloading of swordfish in its own ports. The Spanish fishing boats were therefore unable to either sell or store their catch in Chilean ports or transfer it to other vessels.

---

[55] On this case, *see* Tullio Treves, *Fragmentation of International Law: the Judicial Perspective*, 23 COMUNICAZIONI E STUDI 821 (2008).

In April 2000, the European Community lodged, on the basis of Article 4.4 of the Dispute Settlement Understanding of the WTO,[56] a request for consultations with the Permanent Mission of Chile, highlighting an "apparent lack of conformity of the above measures with Chilean obligations under the General Agreement on Tariffs and Trade 1994," and arguing in particular that "the measures would appear to be in breach of Articles V and XI" of that Agreement.[57] Having failed to reach a solution to the problem, in November of the same year the European Community requested, on the basis of Article 6 of the DSU, the formation of a Panel to adjudicate on the conformity of the Chilean measures with Articles V:1-3 and XI:1 of the GATT.[58]

---

[56] *Understanding on rules and procedures governing the settlement of disputes*, Annex 2 of the WTO Agreement, Uruguay Round, 1986-1994.

[57] WT/DS193/1 of 26 April 2000.

[58] WT/DS193/2 of 7 November 2000. Article V:1-3 of the GATT provides as follows: "*Freedom of Transit* 1. Goods (including baggage), and also vessels and other means of transport, shall be deemed to be in transit across the territory of a contracting party when the passage across such territory, with or without trans-shipment, warehousing, breaking bulk, or change in the mode of transport, is only a portion of a complete journey beginning and terminating beyond the frontier of the contracting party across whose territory the traffic passes. Traffic of this nature is termed in this article "traffic in transit". 2. There shall be freedom of transit through the territory of each contracting party, via the routes most convenient for international transit, for traffic in transit to or from the territory of other contracting parties. No distinction shall be made which is based on the flag of vessels, the place of origin, departure, entry, exit or destination, or on any circumstances relating to the ownership of goods, of vessels or of other means of transport. 3. Any contracting party may require that traffic in transit through its territory be entered at the proper custom house, but, except in cases of failure to comply with applicable customs laws and regulations, such traffic coming from or going to the territory of other contracting parties shall not be subject to any unnecessary delays or restrictions and shall be exempt from customs duties and from all transit duties or other charges imposed in respect of transit, except charges for transportation or those commensurate with administrative expenses entailed by transit or with the cost of services rendered." Article XI:1, on the other hand, establishes the "*General Elimination of Quantitative Restrictions.* 1. No prohibitions or restrictions other than duties, taxes or other charges, whether made effective through quotas, import or export licenses or other measures, shall be instituted or maintained by any contracting party on the importation of any product of the territory of any other contracting

In December 2000, Chile – with the consent of the European Community – made a request to the International Tribunal for the Law of the Sea (ITLOS) for the formation, under Article 15(2) of the Statute of the ITLOS, of a Special Chamber in order to ascertain, amongst other things, whether the Community had observed its own obligations of cooperation and relating to the conservation of swordfish under Articles 64 and 116-119 of the UN Convention on the Law of the Sea (UNCLOS),[59] in respect of the fishing activities of the boats of EU Member States in the area of the high seas adjacent to the Chilean exclusive economic zone.[60] The EC, in turn, requested that the same tribunal find Chile in violation of a number of its obligations under the UNCLOS, in particular Articles 87, 89 and 116-119.[61]

Two different procedures, before two different judicial bodies (the WTO Panel and the Special Chamber of the ITLOS), with regard to two different orders of global norms (those regulating

---

party or on the exportation or sale for export of any product destined for the territory of any other contracting party."

[59] Article 64 of the UNCLOS provides: "1. The coastal State and other States whose nationals fish in the region for the highly migratory species listed in Annex I shall cooperate directly or through appropriate international organizations with a view to ensuring conservation and promoting the objective of optimum utilization of such species throughout the region, both within and beyond the exclusive economic zone. In regions for which no appropriate international organization exists, the coastal State and other States whose nationals harvest these species in the region shall cooperate to establish such an organization and participate in its work." Articles 116-119 concern the "Conservation and management of the living resources of the high seas," and regulate the "Right to fish on the high seas" (Art. 116); the "Duty of States to adopt with respect to their nationals measures for the conservation of the living resources of the high seas" (Art. 117); the "Cooperation of States in the conservation and management of living resources" (Art. 118); and the "Conservation of the living resources of the high seas" (Art. 119).

[60] ITLOS, *Case concerning the conservation and sustainable exploitation of swordfish stocks in the south-eastern Pacific Ocean*, 20 December 2000.

[61] Article 87 of the UNCLOS regulates the "Freedom of the high seas;" while Article 89 establishes the "Invalidity of claims of sovereignty over the high seas."

trade and those regulating fishing), were thus initiated to resolve the same dispute.

In 2001, the EC and Chile reached an agreement with a view to conclude a further, final agreement that would provide an amicable solution to the dispute.[62] In the first agreement, the parties set up a bilateral cooperation scheme for the fishing of swordfish in the south-eastern Pacific, with the creation of a specific body, the EC/Chile Bilateral Scientific and technical Commission (BSTC).[63] The two proceedings, initiated within the frameworks of the WTO and the ITLOS respectively, were suspended at the point at which the bilateral cooperation body was established until the conclusion of the final agreement under the auspices of the Commission.[64]

There are five main aspects of this controversy that are of interest to us here. The first concerns the involvement of two distinct global regimes (regulating trade and fisheries respectively), and a national legal order (Chile). The second is the different parties to the dispute: a number of States (in particular Chile and Spain) and a supranational entity (the European Community). The third con-

---

[62] The text of the agreement is attached to the Communication of the European Community to the WTO Panel of 6 April 2001 (WT/DS193/3).

[63] The program became operational in March 2001. The duties of the Commission are listed in the agreement, and are both of a technical-scientific and a "political" nature (the latter in the sense of promoting cooperation between the parties).

[64] Regarding the proceedings before the WTO Panel, see WT/DS193/3/Add. 1 of 19 April 2001, WT/DS193/3/Add. 2 of 17 November 2003, WT/DS193/3/Add. 3 of 22 December 2005 and WT/DS193/3/Add. 4 of 17 December 2007. For the proceedings before the Special Chamber of ITLOS, see the four Orders of the Tribunal, through which it more than once suspended the proceedings before it (published at http://www.itlos.org/start2_en.html). In the last order, of 11 December 2008, the proceedings were suspended until January 2010, with a view to the conclusion of the final agreement between the parties at some point in 2009. And indeed, in July 2008, the European Commission initiated a series of meetings with the representative of the Government of Chile in order to begin elaborating the final agreement. See http://trade.ec.europa.eu/doclib/docs/2007/may/tradoc_134652.pdf.

cerns the two appellants, the EC within the framework of the WTO on the one hand, and Chile before the ITLOS on the other. The fourth relates to the interests in play in the dispute: the production/ trade interest in the free movement of goods on the one hand, and the protection of living species on the other. The fifth and final element of this controversy is that of the arbiters chosen: the EC, seeking to protect the free movement of goods, requested the institution of a WTO Panel; Chile, whose interest was in the safeguarding of a living species, sought instead the formation of a Special Chamber of the ITLOS.

II. THE *VLORA* DISPUTE

The *Vlora* affair concerned a dispute over the construction of a thermo-electric power plant in the Vlora Gulf, on the Albanian coast. The construction of the power plant (whose production capacity was to be increased threefold at a later date) had been financed by the International Development Association (IDA),[65] the European Bank for Reconstruction and Development (ERD) and by the European Investment bank (EIB).

On the 27th of April 2005, a group made up of residents of the Albanian town who opposed the construction of the plant, the Alliance for the Protection of the Vlora Gulf,[66] filed a complaint with the Compliance Committee of the UN Economic Commission for Europe (UNECE), within the framework of the Aarhus Convention,[67] seeking a finding that the Albanian administration had violated a

---

[65] This organization is part of the World Bank system.

[66] This group changed its name on a number of occasions during the course of the dispute. It is currently named the "Civic Alliance for the Protection of the Bay of Vlora."

[67] *See* http://www.unece.org/env/pp/.

number of Convention provisions (namely Articles 3(2), 6(2) and 7) in the procedure that resulted in the decision to construct the thermo-electric power plant.[68] Article 3(2) states that "each party shall endeavor to ensure that officials and authorities assist and provide guidance to the public in seeking access to information, in facilitating participation in decision making and in seeking access to justice in environmental matters." Article 6(2) provides that "the public concerned shall be informed, either by public notice or individually as appropriate, early in environmental decision-making procedure, and in an adequate, timely and effective manner, inter alia, of: a) the proposed activity and the application on which a decision will be taken…;" furthermore, Article 7 obliges each party to "make appropriate practical and/or other provisions for the public to participate during the preparation of plans and programmes relating to the environment, within a transparent and fair framework, having provided the necessary information to the public."

On the 26th of March 2007, the Compliance Committee presented its proposed decision (its so-called "draft findings and recommendations") to the Meeting of the Parties (MoP).[69] During its meeting from the 13th to the15th of June of the same year, the MoP confirmed that Albania had violated its obligations under the provisions of the Convention.[70] In an "addendum" of March 2008, the Compliance Committee recognized that Albania had adopted a number of measures in order to fulfill its obligations under the Convention, and made a new set of recommendations.[71]

---

[68] The text of the communication is available at www.unece.org/env/pp/compliance/C2005-12/Communication/communication.pdf.

[69] The text of the draft findings can be consulted at www.unece.org/env/pp/compliance/C2005-12/Draft%20findings%20ALB%20v%202007.03.26.pdf.

[70] The decision can be found at www.unece.org/env/documents/2007/pp/ECE_MP.PP_C_1_2007_4_Add_1.pdf.

[71] Point 8 of the Report reads as follows: "[t]he Committee recommends to the Meeting of the Parties, pursuant to paragraph 35 of the annex to decision I/7 and taking into

Parallel to the proceedings before the Compliance Committee, the Alliance – evidently unsatisfied with its success in that forum – brought a claim before the World Bank Inspection Panel in order to establish whether the environmental impact assessment relating to the construction of the thermo-electric plant had been conducted in conformity with Albanian law, Community law and the rules of the World Bank.[72] The claim did not specify precisely which global norms were alleged to have been violated; it did, however, contain a general reference to the Bank's "Operational Policies on Environmental Assessment," to the "Definitions" contained in the Operational Policies, and to the Bank's "Policy on Disclosure of Information"[73] (these are provisions that regulate the procedure to be followed in conducting environmental impact assessments, and the rights of the public to participation and to information within the framework of such assessments).

In its report of the 2nd of June 2007, the Inspection Panel held the Alliance's complaint to be admissible, as it was compatible with the eligibility criteria, and recommended to the Board of Executive

---

account the cause and degree of non-compliance as well as measures taken by the Party concerned in the intersessional period, to: (a) Endorse the original findings and recommendations of the Committee as adopted at its sixteenth meeting; (b) Welcome progress made by the Party concerned in implementing the Committee's recommendations since their adoption in June 2007; (c) Invite the Government of Albania to submit to the Committee periodically (in November 2008, November 2009 and November 2010) information on the progress in implementing the recommendations of the Committee; (d) Request the secretariat, and invite relevant international and regional organizations and financial institutions, to provide advice and assistance to the Party concerned as necessary in the implementation of these measures; (e) Undertake to review the situation at its fourth meeting." (Available at www.unece.org/env/documents/2008/pp/mop3/ece_mp_pp_2008_5_add_1_e.pdf).

[72]http://siteresources.worldbank.org/EXTINSPECTIONPANEL/Resources/Request_for_Inspection.pdf.

[73] These documents are available at http://wbln0018.worldbank.org/institutional/manuals/opmanual.nsf/textonly.

Directors that an investigation into the object of the complaint be conducted.[74]

Again, there are five principal characteristics of this controversy. Firstly, it involves two global regimes – those of the environment (the Aarhus Convention) and the World Bank – and the Albanian national legal order. Secondly, the parties to the dispute are a non-governmental organization, a national government (Albania) and four global or supranational organizations from the economic/financial sector. Thirdly, there is only one claimant: the Alliance for the Protection of the Vlora Gulf. The fourth characteristic is the juxtaposition between a "productive" interest (the production of electricity) and a "protective" one (the protection of the environment). Lastly, the claimant brought the dispute before two different extra-State quasi-judicial bodies, which have a number of characteristics in common with courts (in that, for example, they resolve disputes, operate according to predetermined procedures providing for adversarial proceedings, and enjoy a certain degree of independence).

The two disputes examined here also display a number of interesting elements in common. Firstly, they both concern local problems that have global implications, insofar as certain extra-state regulatory regimes are applicable to national actions; these regimes, in turn, come into conflict with each other (in the first case, commercial regulations "against" those relating to the protection of the sea; in the second, the regulations governing World Bank funding "against" the rules relating to environmental protection).

---

[74] The Panel's Report is available at http://siteresources.worldbank.org/EXTINSPEC-TIONPANEL/Resources/AlbaniaEligibReportFINAL.pdf. The Panel's representatives initiated the investigation in January 2008.

The second commonality is the involvement of conflicting legal orders located at different levels. In both cases the applicants sought to use to their own advantage the fragmentation, or sectoral nature, of different State and extra-State regulatory regimes, appealing to those that best protected their own interests.

The third common element is the quasi-judicial nature of the bodies to which the parties had recourse in seeking a resolution to the disputes: the WTO Panel, the Special Chamber of the ITLOS, the Compliance Committee of the regulatory system established by the Aarhus Convention, and the World Bank Inspection Panel. These extra-State disputes are not, then, to be resolved by armed conflict or ambassadorial intervention, but rather by men in robes – the members of judicial bodies. In short, there has been a turn to the "least dangerous branch" (to use the term coined by Alexander Hamilton in *The Federalist No. 78*)[75] of public power: in the resolution of the controversies analyzed above, neither executive nor legislative authorities were involved.

The fourth common element concerns the sectoral nature of the extra-State bodies to which the parties had recourse in seeking a resolution to the disputes. Both disputes were brought before more

---

[75] Hamilton argued that "[w]hoever attentively considers the different departments of power must perceive, that, in a government in which they are separated from each other, the judiciary, from the nature of its functions, will always be the least dangerous to the political rights of the Constitution; because it will be least in a capacity to annoy or injure them. The Executive not only dispenses the honors, but holds the sword of the community. The legislature not only commands the purse, but prescribes the rules by which the duties and rights of every citizen are to be regulated. The judiciary, on the contrary, has no influence over either the sword or the purse; no direction either of the strength or of the wealth of the society; and can take no active resolution whatever. It may truly be said to have neither FORCE nor WILL, but merely judgment; and must ultimately depend upon the aid of the executive arm even for the efficacy of its judgments." THE FEDERALIST NO. 78 (Alexander Hamilton) (1788). This text has inspired numerous works of US constitutional law; *see, e.g.*, ALEXANDER M. BICKEL, THE LEAST DANGEROUS BRANCH (1986).

than one judge at the same time, precisely because no single body had general competence of the sort that could guarantee the protection of all the interests involved.[76]

---

[76] It is in this sense that the claim by Tullio Treves in the context of the *Swordfish* controversy, that "...neither of the two available dispute settlement mechanisms could cover the whole of the 'real dispute'" can be interpreted. *See* Treves, *supra* note 55, at 862.

CHAPTER IV

THE JUDGE-MADE ORDER

INDEX

I. "JUDICIAL DIALOGUE"

NATIONAL and global legal orders, as illustrated above, sometimes converge; more often, however, they diverge – and turn, in cases of conflict, to bodies that are judicial in nature for their resolution. We must, then, at this point, inquire as to how these bodies decide conflicts. Are they concerned only with the specific case before them or do they, conscious of the absence of a "connective tissue" holding this atomized universe together, also seek to establish general rules for coexistence between legal orders?

The central focus of this inquiry is, as already noted, the different methods employed by judges for the regulation of the relations between legal orders. This issue does not concern the relations between national orders alone, which have already been the subject of numerous studies.[77] The problem that I will examine in what follows covers both the relations between national, supranational and global legal orders (a vertical dimension) and those between different global legal orders (a horizontal dimension). Examining these different types of relations side by side will enable us to draw more general – and more interesting – lessons for the future.

---

[77] *See, e.g.*, the work of Anne-Marie Slaughter, who has analyzed regulation developed by national courts (Anne-Marie Slaughter, *A Global Community of Courts*, 44 HARV. INT'L L.J. 191 (2003)); or that of Julie Allard and Antoine Garapon, who have highlighted the emergence of a "society of courts," and of judge-lieutenants and judge-ambassadors (JULIE ALLARD & ANTOINE GARAPON, LA MONDIALIZZAZIONE DEI GIUDICI. NUOVA RIVOLUZIONE DEL DIRITTO 5 (2006)).

An investigation of this sort can also enable us to ascertain the degree to which the process of "denationalization of law" (i.e., the "movement" of law beyond the frontiers of the State) has developed; to examine by which methods – and not with which results – judges operate as decision-makers of final instance on the different legal levels, building "bridges" between orders; to consider the interaction between the fragmentation of global regulatory regimes and the proliferation of courts; and to discern whether the conditions for the formation of a "general global law" are yet in existence.[78]

As noted at the outset, I am not concerned here with the definition of the principles of law affirmed by courts in the concrete cases before them, but rather with the modalities of elaboration and implementation of the different methods, capable of more general application, used in resolving conflicts between legal orders. That is to say, I am looking for rules of coexistence, "bridges" or linkages between such orders, created and implemented by judges. I am not interested in dialogue between courts in itself, but rather in the means by which judges establish connections between orders. In other words, the work of judges is analyzed here as a "link" between different legal regimes, in the absence of general norms that regulate these relations.[79] In this study, then, I focus on the norms regulating

---

[78] Not to mention allowing us to ascertain whether the theory of Santi Romano, set out in the second part of his *L'ordinamento giuridico*, has been realized in practice.

The major studies on the problem of the relations between legal orders and the role of courts in this are Santi Romano, L'ordinamento giuridico 85 ff. (2d ed. 1977), the two works mentioned above by Yuval Shany, The Competing Jurisdictions of International Courts and Tribunals, *supra* note 9, and Regulating Jurisdictional Relations between National and International Courts, *supra* note 9; Jenny S. Martinez, *Towards an International Judicial System*, 56 Stan. L. Rev. 429 (2003); Treves, *supra* note 55; Filippo Fontanelli & Giuseppe Martinico, *Alla ricerca della coerenza: Le tecniche del 'dialogo nascosto' fra i giudici nell'ordinamento costituzionale multi-livello*, Rivista trimestrale di diritto pubblico 351 (2008).

[79] On this point, *see* Cassese,, *supra* note 2, at 609-626.

the interaction between many legal orders that have been identified by the courts of those orders themselves.

Before beginning, however, it may be useful to recall briefly the general context within which this study is situated. The problem stems from the absence of a general, pre-established hierarchy between legal orders; judges must, therefore, operate without general rules. It is connected, secondly, with the intrinsic weakness of the executive power of the State, which, as a rule, is charged with the management of foreign affairs. The foreign policy power of national executives is, for example, becoming less and less "exclusive" (think, for instance, of the recent creation of the European Arrest Warrant, in which a central role is given to judges and legislators, but not to governments); governments and parliaments are absent at the global level, whereas many extra-State quasi-judicial bodies already exist;[80] and national executives cannot intervene in the horizontal relations between global regimes.

Some have referred to the creation by judges of relations between legal orders as a "judicial dialogue" or "conversation." These terms can, however, create misunderstandings. Courts cannot, in fact, cooperate in resolving the cases brought before them. Informal contacts exist, but these do not fall within the normal conduct of judicial activity as courts cannot initiate processes *ex officio* (they have only a "passive role");[81] these processes are subject to procedural limitations and the decisions resulting from them cannot be of general applicability.

---

[80] It might be argued that the secretariats of international organizations represent forms of extra-state executive power. It should be noted, however, that these are, in reality, usually merely support organs; only in a very few cases do they constitute genuine executives or governments.

[81] Even if, through their decisions, they "govern" the demand for justice, accepting or rejecting requests for intervention.

For the purposes of this analysis, I have selected five different groups or types of cases. The first, which includes the *Simmenthal* case of the European Court of Justice,[82] Opinion No. 1/2004 of the Spanish *Tribunal Constitucional*,[83] and Judgment K 18/04 of the Polish Constitutional Tribunal,[84] concerns the relations between legal orders in the vertical dimension (between the Community legal order and those of its Member States in particular). The second, which includes the *Handyside* case of the European Court of Human Rights[85] and Judgments No. 348 and 349/2007 of the Italian Constitutional Court,[86] also concerns relations between orders in the vertical dimension, but this time between the Council of Europe and national legal orders. The third type of case is exemplified by the *Bosphorus* case of the European Court of Human Rights,[87] and concerns the interaction between two supranational legal orders: the European Community and the Council of Europe. The fourth group, consisting of the decision of the Arbitral Tribunal established under Article 287 of the UNCLOS in the *Mox Plant* case,[88] Decision C-495/03 of the European Court of Justice of the 30th of March 2006, and the *Kadi* judgment by the same court,[89] concerns the relation between global and supranational legal orders (the latter here represented by the EC). The fifth type, exemplified by the *Loewen* case before an ICSID Arbitral Tribunal,[90] concerns the relations between supranational (NAFTA) and national legal orders (those of the State of Mississippi and the United States).

---

[82] ECJ, *Simmenthal v. Italy*, case C-106/77 (28 June 1978).

[83] Judgment DTC 1/2004 (13 December 2004).

[84] Judgment K 18/04 (11 May 2004).

[85] ECtHR, *Case of Handyside v. The United Kingdom*, No. 5493/1972 (7 December 1976).

[86] Constitutional Court Judgments No. 348 and 349/2007 (24 October 2007).

[87] ECtHR, *Case of Bosphorus Hava Yollari Turizm Ve Ticaret Anonim Sirketi v. Ireland*, No. 45036/98 (30 June 2005).

[88] Permanent Court of Arbitration (*ex* art. 287 UNCLOS), *The Mox Plant Case. Ireland v. United Kingdom* (24 June 2003).

[89] ECJ Grand Chamber, *Kadi v Council and Commission* and *Yusuf and Al Barakaat International Foundation v Council and Commission*, Cases C-402/05 P and C-415/05 P (3 September 2008).

[90] ICSID, *The Loewen Group et. al. v. United States of America*. Case No. ARB(AF)/98/3 (26 June 2003).

II. THE EUROPEAN COURT OF JUSTICE'S *SIMMEN-THAL* JUDGMENT: THE PRIMACY OF EUROPEAN OVER NATIONAL LAW

The judgment of the ECJ in the *Simmenthal* case is well known.[91] It is here that the judges established the general principle of the primacy of Community law. This principle does not entail the invalidity of incompatible national laws, but simply treats such laws as non-applicable, even if they were enacted subsequent to the European norm in question.[92]

The most important passages of the judgment are those in which the Court formulated a number of rules on the relationship between Community law and the national laws of Member States (from ¶ 13 onwards). The Court reasoned in the following manner: first of all, the notion of direct applicability of Community norms within the national legal orders of Member States means that the former must be given "full effect." The Court made reference not to the validity of the norms, but rather to their "effectiveness," on the basis of a principle of "conformity" (¶ 14).

---

[91] There exists a vast literature on the *Simmenthal* case. See, in particular, Mario Berri, *Brevi riflessioni sulla "lezione" della Corte comunitaria*, I GIURISPRUDENZA ITALIANA 1153 (1978); Francesco D. Riccioli, *Preoccupanti contrasti tra Corte comunitaria e Corte Costituzionale*, IV IL FORO ITALIANO 204 (1978); Nicola Catalano, *I mezzi per assicurare la prevalenza dell'ordinamento comunitario sull'ordinamento interno*, I GIUSTIZIA CIVILE 816 (1978); Paolo Barile, *Un impatto tra il diritto comunitario e la Costituzione italiana*, I GIURISPRUDENZA COSTITUZIONALE 641 (1978); Luigi Condorelli, *Il caso Simmenthal e il primato del diritto comunitario: due corti a confronto*, I GIURISPRUDENZA COSTITUZIONALE 669 (1978); Sergio M. Carbone & Federico Sorrentino, *Corte di giustizia o corte federale delle Comunità europee?*, I GIURISPRUDENZA COSTITUZIONALE 654 (1978); Giuseppe Sperduti, *La prevalenza, in caso di conflitto, della normativa comunitaria sulla legislazione nazionale*, RIVISTA TRIMESTRALE DI DIRITTO PUBBLICO 3 (1979).

[92] It should be noted that this "non-applicability" is distinct from "disapplication," which concerns only administrative acts.

Secondly, the judges noted that the "full effect" of Community norms can only be achieved through their uniform application within Member States, from the date of their entry into force onwards (¶ 14).

Thirdly, Community norms are a direct source of rights and obligations for all those affected thereby (including Member States, individuals and judges) (¶ 15 and ¶16).

Fourthly, in virtue of the principle of the primacy of Community law, the relationship between provisions of the EC Treaty and directly applicable measures of the Community institutions on the one hand, and the national law of the Member States on the other, is such that those provisions and measures not only render inapplicable *ipso iure* any conflicting provision of current national law, but also preclude the adoption of new national legislative measures where these would be incompatible with Community provisions.

Fifthly, any recognition that national legislative measures that encroach upon the spheres within which the Community exercises legislative power had any legal effect would amount to a denial of the effectiveness of obligations undertaken unconditionally and irrevocably by Member States, and would thus call into question the very foundations of the Community legal order. It is in this sense, for example, that Article 234 of the EC Treaty, which contains rules on references for preliminary rulings,[93] should be interpreted. Indeed,

---

[93] Article 234 of the EC Treaty provides as follows: "The Court of Justice shall have jurisdiction to give preliminary rulings concerning: (a) the interpretation of this Treaty; (b) the validity and interpretation of acts of the institutions of the Community and of the ECB; (c) the interpretation of the statutes of bodies established by an act of the Council, where those statutes so provide. Where such a question is raised before any court or tribunal of a Member State, that court or tribunal may, if it considers that a decision on the question is necessary to enable it to give judgment, request the Court of Justice to give a ruling thereon. Where any such question is raised in a case pending before a court or tribunal of a Member State against whose decisions there is no judicial remedy under

the fact that provision has been made for references by national judges to an appropriate judicial body (the European Court of Justice) in cases of incompatibility between internal and Community rules, in order that the latter body verify the "conventionality"[94] of the contrasting national rule, itself implies recognition of the special nature and superiority of Community law.

It is worth noting that in this judgment (and, in particular, in ¶¶ 20-24), the Court clarifies the doctrine of direct effect and applicability of Community legislation without ever mentioning the validity of conflicting "inferior" rules.[95]

---

national law, that court or tribunal shall bring the matter before the Court of Justice."

[94] The "principle of conventionality" comes from French legal doctrine, referring to the constitutionality of domestic norms with respect to the European Treaties.

[95] These paragraphs of the judgment read as follows: "20. The effectiveness of that provision would be impaired if the national court were prevented from forthwith applying Community law in accordance with the decision or the case-law of the Court; 21. It follows from the foregoing that every national court must, in a case within its jurisdiction, apply Community law in its entirety and protect rights which the latter confers on individuals and must accordingly set aside any provision of national law which may conflict with it, whether prior or subsequent to the Community rule; 22. Accordingly any provision of a national legal system and any legislative, administrative or judicial practice which might impair the effectiveness of Community law by withholding from the national court having jurisdiction to apply such law the power to do everything necessary at the moment of its application to set aside national legislative provisions which might prevent Community rules from having full force and effect are incompatible with those requirements which are the very essence of Community law; 23. This would be the case in the event of a conflict between a provision of Community law and a subsequent national law if the solution of the conflict were to be reserved for an authority with a discretion of its own, other than the court called upon to apply Community law, even if such an impediment to the full effectiveness of Community law were only temporary; 24. The first question should therefore be answered to the effect that a national court which is called upon, within the limits of its jurisdiction, to apply provisions of Community law is under a duty to give full effect to those provisions, if necessary refusing of its own motion to apply any conflicting provision of national legislation, even if adopted subsequently, and it is not necessary for the court to request or await the prior setting aside of such provision by legislative or other constitutional means."

III. DECLARATION NO. 1/2004 OF THE SPANISH *TRIBU-NAL CONSTITUCIONAL*: THE DIFFERENCE BETWEEN SUPREMACY AND PRIMACY

In 2004, the Spanish Constitutional Court[96] was called upon to rule on the ratification of the Treaty containing the text of the European Constitution.[97] Article 95(2) of the Spanish Constitution provides that either the Government or one of the two legislative chambers can request a declaration from the Tribunal as to whether there exists a contradiction between a given clause of an international treaty and the Constitution.[98] Article 93 provides that authorization may be granted, by means of an organic law, for the conclusion of treaties that attribute to an international organization or institution the exercise of competences derived from the Constitution. Moreover, the same provision establishes that it is the responsibility either of Parliament or of the Government, depending on the case in question, to guarantee compliance with these treaties and the resolutions emanating from the international or supranational organizations to which these competences have been devolved.[99]

---

[96] An analysis of this case is contained in Fontanelli & Martinico, *supra* note 78.

[97] The first project for a European Constitution was contained in a Treaty signed in Rome in 2004 (Treaty establishing a Constitution for Europe, Brussels, 13 October 2004). The more recent Treaty of Lisbon of 13 December 2007 modified the original text in a number of ways, among which was the elimination of any reference to the constitutional nature of the Treaty.

[98] Article 95 of the Spanish Constitution provides as follows: "*1. La celebración de un tratado internacional que contenga estipulaciones contrarias a la Constitución exigirá la previa revisión constitucional. 2. El Gobierno o cualquiera de las Cámaras puede requerir al Tribunal Constitucional para que declare si existe o no esa contradicción.*"

[99] The text of Article 93 is as follows: "*Mediante ley orgánica se podrá autorizar la celebración de tratados por los que se atribuya a una organización o institución internacional el ejercicio de competencias derivadas de la Constitución. Corresponde a las Cortes Generales o al Gobierno, según los casos, la garantía del cumplimiento de estos tratados y de las resoluciones emanadas de los organismos internacionales o supranacionales titulares de la cesión.*"

On the basis, then, of Article 95(2) of the Spanish Constitution, and in order to fulfill its responsibilities under Article 93, the Spanish Government asked the *Tribunal Constitucional* to examine whether there was any contradiction between the provisions of the Constitution and those of the European Treaty (in particular Article I-6).[100]

The Declaration of the Constitutional Court was – as the Court itself noted – a decision of "anticipatory jurisdictional defense" or, in other words, a preliminary judgment of a "precautionary" – if both judicial and binding – nature.[101] It was, therefore, an "abstract" judgment in that it related to norms that were not yet in force.

The Court set out its reasoning in four points. Firstly, it observed that European law must assert its own primacy, and that the assertion of this superiority presents itself as an "existential requirement" [*exigencia existencial*]. In other words, the existence of European law depends upon the recognition of its primacy.

Secondly, the Court noted that European law contains the principle of respect for the identities and the laws of Member states, guaranteeing the existence of national legal orders, and respecting their values, principles and fundamental rights.[102]

Thirdly, the Court observed that European law was not general and all-inclusive in nature. It applies only in the spheres of compe-

---

[100] Article I-6 establishes that "the Constitution and law adopted by the institutions of the Union in exercising competences conferred on it shall have primacy over the law of the Member States." The other Articles of the Treaty indicated in the reference were II-111 and II-112, relating to fundamental rights.

[101] On this issue, *see* Paragraph 2, Point 1 of the Opinion: "*...Se si prefiere, al cometido jurisdiccional proprio de este Tribunal se le añade, en virtud de su ejercicio preventivo, una dimensión cautelar al servicio de la salvaguardia de la responsabilidad internacional del Estado...*"

[102] See Articles I-2 and I-5 of the Treaty establishing a Constitution for Europe.

tence of the Union, ceded by States in the exercise of their sovereignty, on the basis of the principle of "attributed competences."[103]

Lastly, the Court declared that no contradiction existed between the primacy of European law and the supremacy of constitutional law, both because the former does not apply in all matters, and because it applies without prejudice to constitutional principles, which thus prevail. The Spanish Constitutional Court thus placed the internal sources system, whose hierarchical structure dictates that constitutional law prevails in cases of conflict, side by side with the different, European normative system. The European system, in turn, prevails over national rules – without, however, supplanting the Constitution, the principles of which it must respect. This reasoning is based upon a distinction between supremacy, understood as a rule of the internal system, on one hand, and primacy, which applies to the European system, on the other.[104]

---

[103] This principle has its basis in the old German doctrine of the "self-limitation" of the State in matters relating to fundamental rights. According to that doctrine, fundamental rights guarantees derive from a self-limiting act of the State, and not from the direct recognition of those rights in citizens.

[104] Indeed, in Paragraph 4 of the declaration, the *Tribunal* established that "supremacy is manifested in the hierarchically superior nature of a given norm, which for that reason becomes the source of legitimacy of the subordinate norms, implying as a result the invalidity of the latter where these are in contravention of its binding provisions. Primacy, on the other hand, does not necessarily entail a hierarchical relationship, but rather a distinction between the sphere of application of different but valid norms, where one or more of these nevertheless has the capacity to displace the others in virtue of a doctrine of preferential application or of prevalence that can be based on a variety of different reasons. In principle, supremacy always implies primacy, excepting cases in which the superior norm has made provision for, in certain areas, its own displacement or inapplicability. The supremacy of the Constitution is, therefore, compatible with rules of application that recognize that preference should be given to norms of an order other than the national one on the condition that the Constitution itself has so provided – which is precisely what happens in Article 93." *See* Angelo Schillaci, *Il tribunale costituzionale spagnolo e la Costituzione europea*, available at www.associazionedeicostituzionalisti.it/cronache/estero/spagna_europa/; Francesco Duranti, *Il tribunal constitucional e la nuova Costituzione europea*, 2005, available at www.forumcostituzionale.it/site/index3.php?option=content&task=view&id=134; Araceli

IV. JUDGMENT K 18/04 OF THE POLISH CONSTITU-TIONAL TRIBUNAL AND ITALIAN CONSTITUTIONAL JURISPRUDENCE: THE DOCTRINE OF "COUNTER-LIMITS"

Judgment K 18/04 of the Polish Constitutional Tribunal concerned Poland's accession to the European Union.[105] Three parliamentary groups from the lower chamber of the Polish Parliament (the Sejm) requested that the Constitutional Tribunal ascertain the conformity of the Treaty concerning the accession of the Republic of Poland to the European Union, read in conjunction with certain provisions of the EC and EU Treaties, with the Polish Constitution. The Tribunal's competence to make this type of judgment is established in and regulated by Article 88 of the Constitution.

The issue confronting the Tribunal was that of the relationship between internal and Community law: if Community law is superior to its internal counterpart, internal rules must conform to those of the Community; how, then, can the problem that arises where Community law is incompatible with the Constitution be resolved? Does Community law or national constitutional law prevail?

Mangas Martín, *La Constitucion y la ley ante el derecho comunitario (Comentario a la sentencia del Tribunal constitucional espanol 28/1991 de 14 de febrero sobre la Ley Orgánica del Régimen Electoral General y el Acta relativa a las elecciones al Parlamento europeo)*, 18 Revista de Insti-tuciones Europeas 587 (1991).

[105] On these cases and the doctrine of counter-limits more generally, *see* Alfonso Celotto & Tania Groppi, *Diritto UE e diritto nazionale: primauté vs controlimiti*, Rivista italiana di diritto pubblico comunitario 1309 (2004); Anneli Albi, *Supremacy of EC Law in the New Member States: Bringing Parliaments into the Equation of "Co-operative Constitutionalism"*, 3 European Constitutional Law Review 25 (2007); Giuseppe Martinico, *Il dialogo fra le corti nell'arena del Gattopardo: l'Europa fra novità costituzionale e nostalgie di comportamento*, *in* Giurisprudenza costituzionale e principi fondamentali. Alla ricerca del nucleo duro delle costituzioni 891 (Sandro Staiano ed., 2005); Giuseppe Martinico, *The Dark Side of the Constitutional Dialogue*, Jean Monnet Working Paper (19-20 May 2008).

The Tribunal set out its reasoning in five main steps. In the first, it affirmed that in cases of irreconcilable conflict between European law and national constitutional law, the latter prevails (¶ 1).

In the second, the Tribunal noted that the European Union only has attributed competences. In this regard, Article 90(1) of the Constitution establishes that Poland can, on the basis of international agreements, "delegate" the competences of the State to international institutions in relation to certain matters.[106]

In the third step, the Court held that the European Union could not take decisions contrary to the Polish Constitution, as Articles 8(1) and 91(3) of the Constitution implicitly establish (¶ 8). The first of these establishes that the Constitution is the supreme law of the country, and the second establishes that the laws created by international organizations have direct applicability and shall prevail over national laws if it is so provided in an international agreement that Poland has ratified.

In its fourth step, the Tribunal emphasized that the Polish Constitution acknowledges the need for cooperation with all Members of the EU (¶ 9), and that European law requires the coexistence between many legal orders; that, in other words, the superior legal order recognizes those inferior to it (¶ 12).

Lastly, the Tribunal concluded that in cases of conflict between a Community norm and the Constitution, the latter prevails, as it its provisions represent a minimum and unsurpassable threshold (¶ 14).

---

[106] In both the provision of the Constitution and the Judgment, the use of the term "delegate" is inappropriate. It refers not to a delegation in the technical sense, which presupposes that the delegating party (in this case, the State) ultimately retains the power to direct the activity in question, but rather to an attribution of competences.

Turning now to Italy, the Italian Constitutional Court has, in a series of decisions in cases of incompatibility between Community norms and the national constitutions, relied upon the doctrine of "counter-limits" (in particular in its decisions No. 183/1973 and 232/1989, and Order No. 454/2006). In the first decision, the Court affirmed that "the idea that such limitations, concretely and precisely defined in the Treaty of Rome (and signed by countries whose legal systems are based upon the principles of the rule of law, and guarantee the essential freedoms of their citizens), could nevertheless grant to the institutions of the EEC an inadmissible power to violate the fundamental principles of our constitutional order or the inalienable rights of the human person, must be rejected."

In its 1989 decision, the Court, after recognizing that the protection of fundamental rights was an integral part of the Community legal order, added that "[t]his, however, does not mean that the competence of this Court to ascertain, by means of an evaluation of the constitutionality of the implementing legislation, whether any provision of the Treaty as interpreted and applied by the Community institutions and organs is in conflict with the fundamental principles of our constitutional order or fails to respect the inalienable rights of the human person can be diminished."

Lastly, in its most recent Order on these issues, the Court established that "national judges must implement fully and immediately those Community laws endowed with direct effect, and refuse to apply, in whole or in part, any internal rules held to be irreconcilable with them, and, where necessary, make a prior preliminary reference to the European Court of Justice under Art. 234 of the EC Treaty;" moreover, the national judge can either hold the incompatible internal rule to be non-applicable, or, if in doubt, "refer to this Court the question of compatibility with the Community legal order of legislation that may impede or prejudice the ongoing observance of the system or essential core principles established by the Treaty, in cases in which it is not possible to arrive at a conforming interpretation and in which the non-application of the internal provision would lead to a clash – justiciable only by the Constitutional Court – with the fundamental principles of the constitutional order or with the inalienable rights of the person."

What emerges from this analysis of the judgment of the European Court of Justice, and those of the Spanish, Polish and Italian Constitutional Courts, is a "flexible" regulation of the boundaries between different legal orders. On the one hand, they affirm, on the basis of the doctrine of primacy, the direct effect of European law, which has an impact on the effects and not the validity of national legislative measures; while, on the other, they also assert the supremacy of the Constitution (not in its entirety, but rather the fundamental principles thereof). Both the doctrines of primacy and of "counter-limits" entail the recognition of a sphere of competence reserved to the State. The acknowledgement of the pre-eminence of European law is, in turn, limited, both by the fact that it is not general in nature, but rather restricted to those matters for which competence has been attributed to the superior level, and by the fact that it impacts upon the effectiveness, and not the validity, of conflicting internal rules.

Both the national and Community courts have arrived at this result, starting from opposite sides and meeting at a point somewhere in the middle. At this point, a boundary line has been drawn; yet it is not definitive, because it is dependent upon the State attribution of competences to the European legal order and on the constitutional principles of each national legal order. In other words, Community law prevails whenever fundamental principles have not been violated; on the contrary, constitutional law prevails whenever the "minimum threshold" has not been observed. The boundary line is not fixed, because it depends on the subject-matter upon which the incompatible internal rule impacts, and on the possible violation by the Community norm of fundamental national principles. The uniformity established by the primacy of European law goes hand in hand with the differentiation accepted by European law from the moment it recognizes the prevalence of constitutional principles that can differ from one Member to another.

In the space of a few decades, then, national and Community courts have succeeded in defining a method that, in the absence of general rules capable of disciplining relations between such orders, nonetheless renders cohabitation possible.[107]

V. THE *HANDYSIDE* CASE BEFORE THE EUROPEAN COURT OF HUMAN RIGHTS: THE MARGIN OF APPRECIATION DOCTRINE

In the *Handyside* judgment,[108] the European Court of Human Rights affirmed for the first time the principle of the "margin of appreciation," which underpins the relations between the legal order of the Council of Europe and those of States Parties to the Convention.

A Danish book, entitled *The Little Red Schoolbook*, was translated and published in the UK. The book dealt with certain delicate

---

[107] I have not taken into consideration here the argument that the doctrine of counter-limits is a mere rhetorical device, deployed in order to hold the State's power to intervene in reserve (and to placate those concerned with the protection of State sovereignty). See generally DIRITTO COMUNITARIO E DIRITTO INTERNO, Proceedings of the Seminar held at the *Palazzo della Consulta*, Rome, 20 April 2007 (2008).

There exists a rich literature on the relations between national and community legal orders. Among recent contributions, see CESARE PAGOTTO, LA DISAPPLICAZIONE DELLA LEGGE (2008), and Oreste Pollicino, *EU Enlargement and European Constitutionalism through the looking glass of the interaction between national and supranational legal system* (unpublished manuscript, on file with the author).

[108] ECtHR, *Case of Handyside v. The United Kingdom*, No. 5493/1972 (7 December 1976).

questions, such as abortion, the use of contraceptives, homosexuality, pornography, pedophilia, etc., offering advice on these issues to youths between the ages of twelve and eighteen.

A number of parent groups demanded the seizure of the book. After an order for seizure had been made by the Director of Public Prosecutions, and an injunction handed down by a Magistrates' Court, Lambeth Magistrates' Court declared the applicant guilty of a violation of the *Obscene Publications Act* of 1959 (as amended in 1964), for having published, for gain, *The Little Red Schoolbook*. According to the English judges, the book had the potential to "deprave and corrupt" adolescents. The Court ordered that Handyside, the publisher, pay a fine and legal costs, and confirmed the seizure and destruction of all copies of the book. This decision was challenged before the Inner London Quarter Sessions, which rejected the appeal and upheld the original decision.

At this point, the English publisher decided to appeal to the European Court of Human Rights, alleging a violation by the English judicial authorities of a series of articles of the ECHR (and in particular Article 10), and seeking "just satisfaction" in accordance with Article 50.

Article 10 of the ECHR provides as follows: "1. Everyone has the right to freedom of expression. This right shall include freedom to hold opinions and to receive and impart information and ideas without interference by public authority and regardless of frontiers. This article shall not prevent States from requiring the licensing of broadcasting, television or cinema enterprises.

2. The exercise of these freedoms, since it carries with it duties and responsibilities, may be subject to such formalities, conditions, restrictions or penalties as are prescribed by law and are necessary in a democratic society, in the interests of national security, territorial integrity or public safety, for the prevention of disorder or crime, for the protection of health or morals, for the protection of the reputation or rights of others, for preventing the disclosure

of information received in confidence, or for maintaining the authority and impartiality of the judiciary."

The relevant part of this provision is that contained in subsection 2, which lists the conditions under which derogations from the freedom of expression are permitted. Any such derogations must be "prescribed by law," and "necessary" in relation to the other interests and fundamental rights explicitly listed. Freedom of expression can, therefore, be limited on the basis of two criteria: one formal (prescription by law) and the other substantive (necessity for the protection of further interests, exhaustively listed in Article 10).

The decision of the Strasbourg Court was set out on the following lines. First of all, the Court emphasized that Article 10 guarantees the right to freedom of expression within the limits established by law and necessary for the protection of morals (¶ 42).

Next, the Court noted that measures derogating from the freedom of expression must be prescribed by law and that, in the present case, the measures in question had been set out in the *Obscene Publications Act* (¶ 44).

Thirdly, the Court considered whether, in the case before it, the requirement of "necessity" established by the ECHR had been met. To this question, it gave a positive response, as the measures relating to the seizure and destruction of the book had been adopted in order to protect morals.

This section of the judgment contains the most interesting elements for our purposes here. The Court held that it could evaluate the appropriateness of the measure to the protection of morals, but intervened only in a subsidiary manner, noting that it was not possible to find in Contracting States a uniform conception of morals. National judges are in a better position to evaluate questions relating to the protection of morals than are their supranational counterparts; therefore, the ECHR leaves to national legislators, administrations and judges a "margin of appreciation" (¶ 48).[109]

The Court insisted, however, that this "margin of appreciation" is not unlimited, as it is subject to a "necessity test" – which consists, in effect, of an examination by the Strasbourg judges of the proportionality of the derogating measure to the ends pursued (¶ 49). The Court further held that it was not its task to take the place of national judges, but rather to evaluate the decisions delivered in the exercise of their "power of appreciation" in the light of the limits established by Article 10, examining also the arguments and evidence adduced at the national level (¶ 50).

At this point, the Court engaged in a long and complex evaluation of the "suitability" and "necessity" of the derogating measures adopted by the English judicial authorities, considering, in the following order: the age of the intended readership of the book; the possibility that the English judges were prejudiced; the appropriateness of the judicial measures to the goal of protecting morals; the temporary nature of the seizure; the characterization of the adoption of derogating measures intended to protect morals, as provided

---

[109] As already noted, this judgment provided the first formulation of the "margin of appreciation" doctrine, defined as the sphere of autonomy and discretion that ("inferior") national legal orders have in relation to the "superior" order of the ECHR, limited by a "necessity test" that translates in practice into the application of a principle of proportionality of means to ends. On the "margin of appreciation," *see* Ignacio de la Rasilla del Moral, *The Increasingly Marginal Appreciation of the Margin-of-Appreciation Doctrine*, 7 GERMAN LAW JOURNAL 611 (2006); Yuval Shany, *Toward a General Margin of Appreciation Doctrine in International Law?*, 16 EUROPEAN JOURNAL OF INTERNATIONAL LAW 907 (2005); Filippo Donati & Pietro Milazzo, *La dottrina del margine di apprezzamento nella giurisprudenza della Corte europea dei diritti dell'uomo*, proceedings of the conference on "*La Corte costituzionale e le corti d'Europa*", Catanzaro, 31 May- 1 June 2002, available at www.associazionedeicostituzionalisti.it/materiali/convegni/copanello020531/donatimilazzo.html; Eyal Benvenisti, *Margin of Appreciation, Consensus, and Universal Standards*, 31 N.Y.U. J. INT'L L. & POL. 843 (1999).

for in Article 10, in terms of a power, and not a general obligation, to act; the absence of any measures taken against the revised edition of the book, which was considered compatible with the requirements of protecting morals, thus indicating the "necessity" of the conduct of the English authorities in relation to the first edition of the text;[110] the irrelevance of the fact that this book, and other publications considered "obscene," were freely circulating in other European States, in which the protection of morals could be based on different standards; and the fact that there was no need for the English authorities to request the modification of the incriminating sections of the text, as Article 10 does not oblige governments to engage in any form of "prior censorship."

At the end of this lengthy reasoning on the "necessity/proportionality" of the measures adopted against Handyside, the Court concluded that the English authorities had not violated Article 10 of the ECHR.

In this case, a relationship between national and supranational judges, and between a national and a supranational order, emerges. According to the Strasbourg Court, the authority that should intervene in questions relating to the protection of morals is the one that is "closest" to the interests involved. The right to freedom of expression is a uniform principle, valid for all of the national legal orders that are part of the Council of Europe, yet each national legislator, judge, and administration enjoys a certain degree of freedom (a "margin of appreciation") in evaluating the necessity of limitations on the freedom guaranteed to all. Such limitations, however, must be proportional and the Strasbourg Court is charged with the task of ensuring that they are so. The intervention of the Court is subsidiary, and consists in an examination of the manner in which national authorities

---

[110] The second edition of the text contained a number of modifications intended to bring it into compliance with the requirements of the protection of morals.

exercise their power to derogate, through the application of the principle of proportionality. The doctrine of "margin of appreciation" is, therefore, closely connected to the principle proportionality.

VI. JUDGMENTS NO. 348 AND 349/2007 OF THE ITALIAN CONSTITUTIONAL COURT: INTERPOSED RULES

In its Judgments 348 and 349 of 2007, the Italian Constitutional Court confronted the problem of the relations between the legal order of the ECHR and that of a State Party to the Convention (Italy), from the perspective of national judges.[111]

In Judgment No. 348, the Court examined the constitutionality of Article 5*bis* (1) and (2) of Decree Law No. 333/1992, converted into law, with adjustments, by Law No. 359/1992,[112] which established the criterion for calculating compensation for expropriation; in Judgment No. 349, the Court evaluated the constitutionality of subsection (7)*bis* of the same legislative instrument, which dealt with damages in cases of illegitimate occupation.[113] In both cases, the

---

[111] The Italian Constitutional Court had already ruled a number of times on the relation between the ECHR system and the national order. Particularly noteworthy in this regard is Judgment No. 10/1993, in which the Court defined the norms of the ECHR as "atypical sources."

[112] Decree Law No. 333 of 11 July 1992 (Emergency Measures for the Improvement of Public Finances), converted, with certain modifications, into Law No. 359 of 8 August 1992.

[113] Articles 5*bis* (1), (2) (7) and (7)*bis* provide as follows: "*1. Fino all'emanazione di un'organica disciplina per tutte le espropriazioni preordinate alla realizzazione di opere o interventi da parte o per conto dello Stato, delle regioni, delle province, dei comuni e degli altri enti pubblici o di diritto pubblico, anche non territoriali, o comunque preordinate alla realizzazione di opere o interventi dichiarati di pubblica utilità, l'indennità di espropriazione per le aree edificabili è determinata a norma dell'articolo 13, terzo comma, della legge 15 gennaio 1885, n. 2892, sostituendo in ogni caso ai fitti coacervati dell'ultimo decennio il reddito dominicale rivalutato di cui agli articoli 24 e seguenti del testo unico delle imposte sui redditi, approvato con d.P.R. 22 dicembre 1986, n. 917. L'importo così determinato è ridotto del 40 per cento; 2. In ogni fase del procedimento espropriativo il soggetto espropriato può convenire la cessione volontaria del bene. In tal caso non si applica la*

measures of constitutionality invoked were Article 111(1) and (2) of the Constitution,[114] in relation to Article 6 of the ECHR, and Article 117(1) of the Constitution,[115] in relation to both Article 6 of the ECHR[116] and Article 1 of Protocol No. 1 to the ECHR.[117]

---

riduzione di cui al comma 1..; 7. Nella determinazione dell'indennità di espropriazione per i procedimenti in corso si applicano le disposizioni di cui al presente articolo; 7-bis. In caso di occupazioni illegittime di suoli per causa di pubblica utilità, intervenute anteriormente al 30 settembre 1996, si applicano, per la liquidazione del danno, i criteri di determinazione dell'indennità di cui al comma 1, con esclusione della riduzione del 40 per cento. In tal caso l'importo del risarcimento è altresì aumentato del 10 per cento. Le disposizioni di cui al presente comma si applicano anche ai procedimenti in corso non definiti con sentenza passata in giudicato."

[114] Articles 111(1) and (2) of the Constitution establish that *"1. La giurisdizione si attua mediante il giusto processo regolato dalla legge. 2. Ogni processo si svolge nel contraddittorio tra le parti, in condizioni di parità, davanti a giudice terzo e imparziale. La legge ne assicura la ragionevole durata"* (1. Jurisdiction is implemented through due process regulated by law. 2. All court trials are conducted with adversary proceedings and the parties are entitled to equal conditions before an impartial judge in third position. The law provides for the reasonable duration of trials).

[115] Article 117(1) of the Constitution provides: *"La potestà legislativa è esercitata dallo Stato e dalle Regioni nel rispetto della Costituzione, nonché dei vincoli derivanti dall'ordinamento comunitario e dagli obblighi internazionali"* (1. Legislative powers shall be vested in the State and the Regions in compliance with the Constitution and with the constraints deriving from EU-legislation and international obligations).

[116] Article 6 of the ECHR reads as follows: "In the determination of his civil rights and obligations or of any criminal charge against him, everyone is entitled to a fair and public hearing within a reasonable time by an independent and impartial tribunal established by law. Judgment shall be pronounced publicly but the press and public may be excluded from all or part of the trial in the interests of morals, public order or national security in a democratic society, where the interests of juveniles or the protection of the private life of the parties so require, or to the extent strictly necessary in the opinion of the court in special circumstances where publicity would prejudice the interests of justice. 2. Everyone charged with a criminal offence shall be presumed innocent until proved guilty according to law. 3. Everyone charged with a criminal offence has the following minimum rights: to be informed promptly, in a language which he understands and in detail, of the nature and cause of the accusation against him; to have adequate time and facilities for the preparation of his defense; to defend himself in person or through legal assistance of his own choosing or, if he has not sufficient means to pay for legal assistance, to be given it free when the interests of justice so require; to examine or have examined witnesses against him and to obtain the attendance and examination of witnesses on his behalf under the same conditions as witnesses against him; to have the free assistance of an interpreter if he cannot understand or speak the language used in court."

[117] Article 1 of the Additional Protocol to the ECHR provides: "Every natural or legal

Both dealt with questions arising from cases brought by the owners of areas of building land that had been expropriated by the administration. They challenged the decision to apply the criterion for the calculation of compensation provided for by the above-mentioned Article 5*bis* instead of that laid down by the old rules governing the issue of expropriation, dating back to the Law of 1865. The new criterion, in contrast with the old one, did not entail the payment of a sum equal to the market value of the property expropriated, but rather of an amount equal to the average of the value of the property and the revalued cadastral income, reduced by 40% (this reduction does not apply in cases in which the property is voluntarily ceded to the Government – where, therefore, the "price" determined by the administration is accepted – or those involving damages paid for illegitimate occupation). The new criterion is much less advantageous to owners than was the older one.[118]

person is entitled to the peaceful enjoyment of his possessions. No one shall be deprived of his possessions except in the public interest and subject to the conditions provided for by law and by the general principles of international law."

[118] These two judgments have been the subject of numerous studies. *See*, in particular, Oreste Pollicino, *Constitutional Court at the crossroads between constitutional parochialism and co-operative constitutionalism. Judgments No. 348 and 349 of 22 and 24 October 2007*, 4 EUROPEAN CONSTITUTIONAL LAW REVIEW 363 (2008); Francesca Biondi Dal Monte & Filippo Fontanelli, *The Decisions No.. 348 and 349/2007 of the Italian Constitutional Court: the Efficacy of the European Convention in the Italian Legal System*, 9 GERMAN LAW JOURNAL 889 (2008); Barbara Randazzo, *Costituzione e Cedu: il giudice delle leggi apre una «finestra» su Strasburgo*, GIORNALE DI DIRITTO AMMINISTRATIVO 25 (2008); Massimo Luciani, *Alcuni interrogativi sul nuovo corso della giurisprudenza costituzionale in ordine ai rapporti tra diritto italiano e diritto internazionale*, CORRIERE GIURIDICO 201 (2008); Roberto Conti, *La Corte costituzionale viaggia verso i diritti CEDU: prima fermata verso Strasburgo*, CORRIERE GIURIDICO 205 (2008); Antonio Ruggeri, *La Cedu alla ricerca di una nuova identità, tra prospettiva formale – astratta e prospettiva assiologico - sostanziale d'inquadramento sistematico* (2007), available at www.forumcostituzionale.it/site/images/stories/pdf/documenti_forum/giurisprudenza/2007/0001_ruggeri_nota_348_349_2007.pdf.; Mario Savino, *Il cammino internazionale della Corte costituzionale dopo le sentenze n. 348 e 349 del 2007*, RIVISTA ITALIANA DI DIRITTO PUBBLICO COMUNITARIO 743 (2008); Claudio Panzera, *Il bello dell'essere diversi. Corte costituzionale e corti europee ad una svolta*, FORUM DI QUADERNI COSTITUZIONALI (2008); Cesare Pinelli, *Sul trattamento giurisdizionale della CEDU e delle leggi con essa confliggenti*, GIURISPRUDENZA COSTITUZIONALE 3518 (2007); Anna Moscarini, *Indennità di espropriazione e valore di mercato*

Prior to the reform of Article 117(1) of the Constitution in 2001, the Constitutional Court had pronounced many times on the legitimacy of Article 5*bis* of Law No. 359/1992, always rejecting the challenge. The provision referred to in these preceding decisions was principally Article 42 of the Constitution. The Strasbourg Court, in decisions handed down in 2004 and 2006, declared that the Italian rules were incompatible with the provisions of the ECHR, constituting a "structural and systematic" violation of the Convention.[119]

In its two 2007 Judgments, the Constitutional Court declared the unconstitutionality of Article 5*bis* (1), (2) and (7)*bis* of the 1992 rules, on the grounds of incompatibility with Article 117(1) of the Constitution.[120] This incompatibility stemmed from the violation by the rules in question of Article 6 of the ECHR and of Article 1 of

del bene: un passo avanti (ed uno indietro) della Consulta nella costruzione del patrimonio costituzionale europeo, GIURISPRUDENZA COSTITUZIONALE 3525 (2007); Marta Cartabia, *Le sentenze "gemelle": diritti fondamentali, fonti, giudici*, GIURISPRUDENZA COSTITUZIONALE 3564 (2007); Andrea Guazzarotti, *La Corte e la CEDU: il problematico confronto di standard di tutela alla luce dell'art. 117, comma 1, Cost.*, GIURISPRUDENZA COSTITUZIONALE 3574 (2007); Vincenzo Sciarabba, *Nuovi punti fermi (e questioni aperte) nei rapporti tra fonti e corti nazionali ed internazionali*, GIURISPRUDENZA COSTITUZIONALE 3579 (2007); Francesca Angelini, *L'incidenza della CEDU nell'ordinamento italiano alla luce di due recenti pronunce della Corte costituzionale*, IL DIRITTO DELL'UNIONE EUROPEA 487 (2008); Maria Eugenia Bartoloni, *Un nuovo orientamento della Corte costituzionale sui rapporti fra ordinamento comunitario e ordinamento italiano?*, IL DIRITTO DELL'UNIONE EUROPEA 511 (2008). On the relations between the Italian legal order and that of the ECHR more generally, see Ugo Villani, *Sul valore della Convenzione europea dei diritti dell'uomo nell'ordinamento italiano*, III STUDI SULL'INTEGRAZIONE EUROPEA 7 (2008). On the relations between European courts, see VINCENZO SCIARABBA, TRA FONTI E CORTI. DIRITTI E PRINCIPI FONDAMENTALI IN EUROPA: PROFILI COSTITUZIONALI E COMPARATI DEGLI SVILUPPI SOVRANAZIONALI (2008) and JUSTICIA CONSTITUCIONAL Y UNIÓN EUROPEA. UNO ESTUDIO COMPARADO DE LAS EXPERIENCIAS DE ALEMANIA, AUSTRIA, ESPAÑA, FRANCIA, ITALIA Y PORTUGAL (Javier Tajadura & Josu de Miguel eds., 2008).

[119] *See*, in particular the case of *Scordino v. Italy*, Application No. 36813/97 (29 March 2006), cited by the Constitutional Court in this judgment.

[120] In its judgment 348/2007, the Court found unconstitutional Articles 37(1) and (2) of the Presidential Decree No. 327 of 8 June 2001 (Consolidated Text of the Laws and Regulations relating to Public Expropriation), which reproduced the provisions of Article 5*bis* of the 1992 law.

the first Additional Protocol to the Convention, which were held to be "interposed rules."[121] The Court held further that ECHR rules should be considered by national judges in the light of the way in which they had been interpreted by the Strasbourg Court (para. 4.6 of Judgment No. 348).

In cases of incompatibility between an internal norm and an ECHR norm, the judge – according to the Constitutional Court – should raise the question of constitutionality, performing a double check to "establish at the same time that both respect the Constitution, and more specifically that the interposed rule is compatible with the Constitution, as well as the constitutionality of the contested provision in the light of the interposed rules" (¶ 4.7 of Judgment No. 348). Thus, the idea that national judges can simply decide not to apply internal rules – which, of course, is the course of action envisaged in cases of conflict with Community rules – is rejected in cases of conflict with the ECHR (¶ 4.3 of Judgment No. 348).

The effect of this "interposition" of international treaty rules is that ordinary national legislation must respect them; but they, in turn, must also respect the Constitution.

---

[121] In particular, the Court held that "[t]he structure of the constitutional provision in relation to which the present question is raised is similar to that of other constitutional provisions, which become applicable *in concreto* when placed in a close relationship to other non-constitutional provisions necessary to give a substantive content to a principle which limits itself to setting out in general terms a quality which the laws referred to in it must possess. The necessary provisions in such cases have a lower status than the Constitution, but higher than ordinary legislation. Although its capacity to designate a unitary category is sometimes disputed, irrespective of the use of the expression "interposed sources," prevalent in academic literature and in a rich series of decisions of this court to indicate this type of provision..., it must be accepted that the principle contained in Article 117(1) of the Constitution becomes operative *in concreto* only if the "international law obligations" which restrict the legislative power of the state and the regions are specified. In the particular case before this court, the principle is supplemented and made operative by the provisions of the ECHR, the role of which in this case is therefore to give substance to the state's international law obligations."

It is interesting to inquire whether the mechanism of interposition, as affirmed by the Court in relation to ECHR norms, could also be applicable to other international treaty norms. There is nothing in the texts of the two Judgments that would exclude the application of the mechanism approved therein to all of the commitments under international treaties, but one difference should be borne in mind. A number of treaties make provision for an appropriate judicial body: the norms of such treaties will be assessed on the basis of the interpretation given to them by those bodies. Other treaties make no provision for a judicial body: the norms of those treaties can be interpreted freely by national judges (in this sense, the national judges in question become also judges of the international norms).

According the interpretation of the Constitutional Court, Article 117(1) of the Constitution thus allows judges to "bring home" the ECHR, and international treaty norms more generally.[122]

It may be useful, at this point, to consider the *Handyside* case and Judgments 348 and 349/2007 together. These come from judges at different levels, one in a "superior" and the other in an "inferior" position (or, perhaps better: one located in a more extensive legal order, the other operating in a legal order that constitutes only part of the first). Both sets of judges are engaged in a "dialogue," in the sense that they are seeking criteria for establishing connections between the legal orders in question.

The judge of the more extensive legal order, interested in ensuring that the principle of uniformity is respected, allows, nevertheless, a certain degree of divergence thanks to the "margin of appreciation" doctrine; however, he retains for himself the final say on the

---

[122] This expression is taken from Harold Hongju Koh, *Bringing International Law Home*, 35 Hous. L. Rev. 623 (1998).

"necessity/proportionality" of the different national laws and their implementation. The judge of the less extensive order also has an interest in ensuring respect for the law common to the more extensive legal space, and to this end he inserts it into his own internal legal order, "nationalizing" it in the process, as the standard for the legitimacy of ordinary laws (in that the rule interposed between the Constitution and the ordinary law must be respected by the latter). This, however, also ensures a dose of divergence, if the Constitution so requires: the interposed rule, while superior to ordinary law, must itself respect the Constitution and constitutional laws, and is thus subordinate to them.

This "creative activity" of judges has therefore generated a set of reusable, indeed permanent, connecting principles between legal orders; this helps to attenuate the negative consequences of the absence of a superior order that encompasses all and establishes a hierarchy between norms.

Taking together the types of connection established by judges between the Community and national legal orders on the one hand, and between the ECHR and national orders on the other, we can identify both analogies and dissimilarities.

In both cases, the absence of a superior order encompassing those at the supranational and national levels creates a void of connecting norms, of rules of recognition, and of hierarchy. In both cases, judges compensate for this by establishing both the principle of respect for uniform, general rules (through the techniques of direct effect and interposition) and the principle of recognition of a sphere of self-determination of the "inferior" legal systems (through the doctrines of "counter-limits" and the margin of appreciation).

However, in the close-knit relations between the national legal orders and that of the Community, diversity is preserved in terms of fundamental constitutional principles alone; by contrast, in the relations between the legal order of the ECHR and those of its State Parties (and between international treaty law and national legal orders more generally), which are less close, the national Constitution in its entirety can be a source of difference.

VII. THE *BOSPHORUS* CASE BEFORE THE EUROPEAN COURT OF HUMAN RIGHTS, AND THE "EQUIVALENT PROTECTION" OF HUMAN RIGHTS

In 1992, Bosphorus, an airline charter company incorporated in Turkey, leased two aircraft from Yugoslav airlines (JAT), the national airline of the former Yugoslavia. The aircraft were owned by JAT, but operated by the Turkish company.

From 1991 onwards, the United Nations (UN) adopted a series of sanctions against the Federal Republic of Yugoslavia, in an attempt to bring an end to the armed conflicts and grave violations of human rights then occurring in that country. One UN Security Council Resolution (No. 820 of 1993) provided that States should impound the aircraft belonging to companies in which a majority or controlling interest was held by Yugoslav natural or legal persons, or those operating in Yugoslavia. This Resolution was implemented in Europe by Regulation (EEC) 990/93, which entered into force on the 28th of April 1993.

In May 1993, one of the two aircraft arrived in Dublin, and was impounded by the Irish Department of Transport. There followed two judicial review proceedings before the Irish High Court, a preliminary reference to the ECJ, and a judgment of the Irish Supreme Court, until July 1997, by which time the lease had ended, an agreement had been reached between JAT and the Irish Department of Transport, and the aircraft was returned to the former.

In 1997, Bosphorus filed a complaint before the European Court of Human Rights, alleging that the impounding of the aircraft was in violation of the right to property guaranteed by Article 1 of the First Protocol to the European Court of Human Rights.

This provides, *inter alia*, that "[e]very natural or legal person is entitled to the peaceful enjoyment of his possessions. No one shall be deprived of his possessions except in the public interest and subject to the conditions provided for by law and by the general principles of international law. The preceding provisions shall not, however, in any way impair the right of a State to enforce such laws as it deems necessary to control the use of property in accordance with the general interest... ."

The Court concluded[123] that Ireland was not in violation of that provision (¶ 167), on the basis of a complex chain of reasoning that can be summarized as follows. States have a wide margin of appreciation in setting limits on the right to property (¶ 149). The actions of the Irish authorities had been taken in order to comply with the provisions of Article 8 of the Community Regulation, and not in the exercise of any discretionary power (¶ 148). Compliance with Community law can be viewed as a "general interest" for the purposes of Article 1 of the Protocol (¶ 150). It is not, however, sufficient that the action in question is taken in pursuance of the general interest; it is also necessary that the rights established in the European Convention on Human Rights, or "equivalent" (in the sense of "comparable") guarantees, are respected. If an equivalent level of protection is provided, then it can be presumed that the State has not departed from the requirements of the Convention (¶ 156). Community law in general ensures a level of protection of fundamental rights equivalent to that provided by the Convention, leading to a presumption that the latter has been respected (¶¶ 159-165).

In this case, the Strasbourg Court adopted an attitude of "deference" with respect to Community law, thus declining to apply Con-

---

[123] ECtHR, *Case of Bosphorus Hava Yollari Turizm Ve Ticaret Anonim Sirketi v. Ireland*, No. 45036/98 (30 June 2005).

vention law. Of more interest to us here, however, is the principle of equivalence, which entails that, where one legal order provides for protection equivalent to that of another, the latter abstains from applying its own norms. This, however, implies that where the first legal order does not offer equivalent protection, the second will intervene in order to ensure respect for the rights that it guarantees. A further, and more important, implication is that, in this way, the two legal orders are construed together as a single, complete whole, in which the level of protection guaranteed cannot be diminished. If it is lowered in the first legal order, the second intervenes.[124]

VIII. THE *MOX PLANT* ARBITRATION UNDER ARTICLE 287 UNITED NATIONS CONVENTION ON LAW OF THE SEA: THE DIVISION OF FUNCTIONS

The *Mox Plant* case concerned the disastrous environmental consequences resulting from the disposition and transportation of radioactive substances from certain British nuclear plants (British Nuclear Fuels, plc),[125] located in Sellafield, which were discharging some eight million liters of nuclear waste into the Irish Sea every day, contaminating the waters and marine fauna.[126] According to estimates by Greenpeace, this stretch of sea is among the most heavily polluted in the world. It is, moreover, a "semi-enclosed" sea in the sense of Article 122 of the UNCLOS.[127]

---

[124] On the *Bosphorus* case, *see* Lech Garlicki, *Cooperation of Courts: The Role of Supranational Jurisdictions in Europe*, 6 INT'L J. CONST. L. 509 (2008). *See also* the case notes on the judgment by Frank Hoffmeister 100 AM. J. INT'L L. 442 (2006) and by Sionaidh Douglas-Scott, 43 COMMON MARKET LAW REVIEW 243 (2006); Fontanelli & Martinico, *supra* note 78, at 351-387.

[125] A company entirely owned by the UK Government.

[126] On the *Mox Plant* case, *see* in particular Nikolaos Lavranos, *The Mox Plant and Ijzeren Rijn Disputes: Which Court is the Supreme Arbiter?*, 19 LEIDEN JOURNAL OF INTERNATIONAL LAW 223 (2006).

[127] United Nations Convention on the Law of the Sea, Montego Bay, 10 December

In 2001, Ireland, no longer prepared to tolerate the consequences of the British pollution, requested the establishment of an Arbitral Tribunal under Article 287 of the UNCLOS, seeking a declaration that the UK had violated its obligations under the Convention and appropriate remedies. In particular, Ireland alleged a violation of Articles 123, 192, 193, 194, 197, 206, 207, 211, and 213 of the Convention. The most relevant of these for our purposes here is Article 123, which deals with relations of cooperation between States bordering enclosed or semi-enclosed seas.[128]

On the 24ᵗʰ of June 2003, the Arbitral Tribunal made an Order entitled "Suspension of Proceedings on Jurisdiction and Merits, and Request for Further Provisional Measures," which referred to the objections raised by the United Kingdom, as respondent in the proceedings, relating to the jurisdiction of the Tribunal. In particular, the UK argued that the dispute may fall within the jurisdiction of the European Court of Justice, involving issues within the competence of the Community. The Tribunal was thus required to make a preliminary judgment as to the competent jurisdiction.

1982. This Convention was negotiated between 1973 and 1982, signed in 1982, and entered into force in 1994, with 159 States Parties. The text is composed of 320 Articles. The Convention substituted the traditional principle of the freedom of the seas with a number of others, relating, for example, to the common use of marine resources, and the management and development of oil-extraction and fishing activities. Article 122 of the UNCLOS, on "definitions," establishes that "[f]or the purposes of this Convention, "enclosed or semi-enclosed sea" means a gulf, basin or sea surrounded by two or more States and connected to another sea or the ocean by a narrow outlet or consisting entirely or primarily of the territorial seas and exclusive economic zones of two or more coastal States."

[128] Article 123 of the UNCLOS provides as follows: "States bordering an enclosed or semi-enclosed sea should co-operate with each other in the exercise of their rights and in the performance of their duties under this Convention. To this end they shall endeavour, directly or through an appropriate regional organization: (a) to co-ordinate the management, conservation, exploration and exploitation of the living resources of the sea; (b) to co-ordinate the implementation of their rights and duties with respect to the protection and preservation of the marine environment; (c) to co-ordinate their scientific research policies and undertake where appropriate joint programmes of scientific research in the area; (d) to invite, as appropriate, other interested States or international organizations to co-operate with them in furtherance of the provisions of this article."

In responding to this objection, the Tribunal noted that, in May 2003, the European Commission gave a Written Answer to the European Parliament,[129] in which it indicated that it was considering the possibility of initiating proceedings against Ireland under Article 226 of the EC Treaty, raising before the European Court of Justice the questions of Community competence in relation to the matters that formed the object of the dispute, and of the exclusive jurisdiction of the European Court (¶ 21).

Next, the Tribunal noted that, although neither party to the dispute had sought to sustain the view that the Court of Justice had exclusive jurisdiction over the issues in question, it could not be said with certainty that this possibility would be rejected by the European judges, thus precluding the jurisdiction of the tribunal under Article 292 of the UNCLOS (¶ 22). That provision, relating to "Obligations under general, regional or bilateral agreements," establishes that ""[i]f the States Parties which are parties to a dispute concerning the interpretation or application of this Convention have agreed, through a general, regional or bilateral agreement or otherwise, that such dispute shall, at the request of any party to the dispute, be submitted to a procedure that entails a binding decision, that procedure shall apply in lieu of the procedures provided for in this Part, unless the parties to the dispute otherwise agree." The UNCLOS system – as yet unperfected – thus envisages a sort of "flexible reference" to other legal orders where these are more developed.

Next, the Tribunal acknowledged that the problems raised in the case concerned the "international operation of a separate legal order" (¶ 24). For this reason, "it would still not be appropriate for the Tribunal to proceed with hearings on the merits in respect

---

[129] Plenary Session of the European Parliament, oral question by Proinsias De Rossa (H-0256/03), Thursday, 15 May 2003.

of any such provisions" (¶ 26), particularly given that there were substantial doubts as to whether the jurisdiction of the Tribunal could be established in respect of all or any of the claims before it. On the other hand, the Tribunal observed that the Community system is certainly a "legal order [that] may involve decisions that are final and binding" (¶ 27); therefore, the applicant would have had a greater chance of satisfaction had the complaint been brought before the European Court of Justice.

The Tribunal thus held that, given the conditions of "mutual respect and comity which should prevail between judicial institutions," it would be "inappropriate" for it to proceed further in the dispute before it, adding that, if it were to make a decision,[130] there was a risk that this could conflict with that reached by the Community judges.

In essence, over and above the preference for a fully judicial solution (a principle established, as noted above, by Art. 282 of the Convention), the Tribunal also affirmed a principle of respect for the separate legal order primarily concerned with the matters that form the object of the dispute. It therefore ordered the suspension of the arbitral proceedings until December 2003.[131]

---

[130] Paragraph 28 of the Order reads as follows: "in the circumstances, and bearing in mind considerations of mutual respect and comity which should prevail between judicial institutions both of which may be called upon to determine rights and obligations as between two States, the Tribunal considers that it would be inappropriate for it to proceed further with hearing the Parties on the merits of the dispute in the absence of a resolution of the problems referred to. Moreover, a procedure that might result in two conflicting decisions on the same issue would not be helpful to the resolution of the dispute between the Parties."

[131] On the 6th of June 2008, the Tribunal adopted Order No. 6 on the definitive "Termination of Proceedings," following notification by Ireland of its withdrawal of its complaint against the UK dated the 15th of February 2007. See http://www.pca-cpa.org/upload/files/MOX%20Plant%20Press%20Release%20Order%20N.%206.pdf.

On the 30th of May 2006, in its judgment C-459/2003,[132] the European Court of Justice ruled on the claim brought by the Commission against Ireland on the basis of Articles 226 of the EC Treaty and 141 of the Euratom Treaty. The Commission had sought a declaration from the Court that Ireland, in initiating dispute resolution proceedings against the UK under the UNCLOS in relation to the Mox plant, had failed to respect it obligations under Articles 10 and 292 of the EC Treaty, and Articles 192-193 of the Euratom Treaty.[133] The Court accepted the arguments of the Commission, finding that Ireland had violated the norms in question.

This case also provides a useful illustration of the manner in which courts operate in defining the relations between different legal orders. Here, neither of the legal orders involved was "statal" in nature; rather, one was global (relating to the law of the sea) and the other supranational (the Community order). The global norm simply established a principle of preference for a fully judicial solution (i.e., a procedure that results in a binding decision) to the dis-

---

[132] ECJ case C-459/03 of 30 May 2006, *European Commission v. Ireland*.

[133] Article 10 of the EC Treaty establishes a principle of "loyal cooperation," providing that "Member States shall take all appropriate measures, whether general or particular, to ensure fulfillment of the obligations arising out of this Treaty or resulting from action taken by the institutions of the Community. They shall facilitate the achievement of the Community's tasks. 2. They shall abstain from any measure which could jeopardise the attainment of the objectives of this Treaty." Article 292 of the EC Treaty can be viewed as symmetrical to Article 282 of the UNCLOS; the former provides that "Member States undertake not to submit a dispute concerning the interpretation or application of the Treaties to any method of settlement other than those provided for therein." Indeed, Article 192 and 193 of the Euratom treaty simply repeat the provisions of Articles 10 and 292 of the EC Treaty: "Member States shall take all appropriate measures, whether general or particular, to ensure fulfillment of the obligations arising out of this Treaty or resulting from action taken by the institutions of the Community. They shall facilitate the achievement of the Community's tasks. They shall abstain from any measure which could jeopardize the attainment of the objectives of this Treaty" (192); and "Member States undertake not to submit a dispute concerning the interpretation or application of this Treaty to any method of settlement other than those provided for therein" (193).

pute. The judicial body here added a further principle, created by judges alone, of respect for the separate legal order primarily concerned with the subject-area of the dispute.

IX. THE *KADI CASE* BEFORE THE EUROPEAN COURT OF JUSTICE, AND THE PRIMACY OF GLOBAL OVER EUROPEAN LAW

Yassin Abdullah Kadi, an international businessman and Saudi Arabian citizen with important financial interests in the European Union, and the Al Barakaat International Foundation, established in Sweden, had all of their funds frozen in the UK and in Sweden respectively. Following unsuccessful attempts to have this reversed before national administrative and judicial bodies, they brought their case before the Court of First Instance of the European Communities, as the British and Swedish authorities had acted in order to give effect to a Community Regulation, itself adopted in implementation of a UN Security Council Resolution, intended to help combat international terrorism. The parties requested that the Court annul the contested Community rules. The Court, however, rejected this request, holding that the resolutions of the Security Council were binding on the Community, whose powers in the matter at issue were limited, having no autonomous discretion in the implementation of the Resolutions in question.

Both parties then appealed the decision of the Court of First Instance, seeking an order for annulment from the European Court of Justice. On the 3rd of September 2008, in its decision in the joined proceedings C-402/05 P and C-415/05 P, the ECJ reversed the judgment of the Court of First Instance and annulled Regulation EC 881/2002 (insofar as it applied to the two appellants), albeit ordering that the effects of the latter could be maintained for a period not exceeding three months from the date of the judgment.

The Court of First Instance had denied the existence of a number of legal principles (such as the right to participate in administrative proceedings, the right to a hearing, the right to property) on the basis of a centralized approach to the relations between the two legal orders, based on the French model:[134] the Community had acted in a purely executive fashion, having no autonomous discretion whatsoever, its powers being circumscribed. Its action, therefore, was immune from the jurisdiction of the Court, and could not be subjected to the requirements of the rule of law (see in particular ¶ 214 and ¶ 231 of the judgment of the Court of First Instance). The Court of Justice, on the other hand, reconfigured the relations between the UN and the European Union, affirming the primacy of the former over the latter in different terms.

The reasoning of the Court of Justice proceeded in five main logical steps. First: UN law has primacy (or prevalence) (¶ 288); thus, it must be respected by Community law (¶ 291 and ¶ 318). Second: global law establishes terms, objectives and obligations (¶¶ 296-297), but does not impose a particular or pre-established model for their implementation, thus leaving a free choice to States

---

[134] Or perhaps an approach viewing them as a "legal pyramid." For a critique of this metaphor, see Armin von Bogdandy, *Pluralism, Direct Effect, and the Ultimate Say: On the Relationship Between International and Domestic Constitutional Law*, 6 INT'L J. CONST. L. 397 (2008). On the ECJ's *Kadi* judgment, see the comments published in 14 GIORNALE DI DIRITTO AMMINISTRATIVO (2008), in particular Aldo Sandulli, *Caso Kadi: tre percorsi a confronto* (1088-1090); Sabino Cassese, *Ordine comunitario e ordine globale* (1091-1092); Edoardo Chiti, *I diritti di difesa e di proprietà nell'ordinamento europeo* (1093-1095); Mario Savino, *Libertà e sicurezza nella lotta al terrorismo: quale bilanciamento?* (1096-1099); Giulio Vesperini, *Il principio del contraddittorio e le fasi comunitarie di procedimenti globali* (1100-1101); Giacinto della Cananea, *Un nuovo nomos per l'ordine globale* (1102-1104). *See also* Grainne de Burca, *The European Court of Justice and the International Legal Order after Kadi*, Jean Monnet Working Paper 01/09, NYU School of Law.

in that regard; the means of implementation are to be determined in accordance with the internal procedure applicable in each national or supranational legal order. Third: a Community regulation implementing global law is a Community act, not one of a subsidiary organ of the UN (¶ 326 and ¶ 314); it is not, therefore, directly attributable to the UN. Fourth: the Community is an autonomous legal order (¶¶ 316-317), constituting a community based on the rule of law (¶¶ 281 ff). Fifth: consequently, in implementing global law, Community law must respect fundamental principles of law.

The complex reasoning of the Court conceals a number of uncertainties, and has a number of hidden implications. Firstly, it is not clear whether the primacy of global law is structural or functional: the Court seems to affirm the latter in Paragraph 294 of its judgment, in which it emphasizes that the UN has the principal responsibility for combating terrorism; by contrast, in Paragraph 305, the relations between legal orders are presented – if only in a hypothetical instance – as a hierarchy of norms. Secondly, the references to global law oscillate: it is the UN Charter that does not impose any particular model for implementation, while it is the Resolutions of the Security Council that establish the obligations relating to the fight against international terrorism: therefore, reference is made both to global "constitutional" or primary law on the one hand, and secondary law on the other. Thirdly, from the Court's reconfiguration of relations between the two legal orders, there follow two limits on the global law in question: it only has primacy on the condition that it limits itself to setting the objectives of anti-terrorism policies (¶¶ 296-297) and that it conforms with the "constitutional" principles of the Community (contained above all in Art. 6(1) of the EU Treaty) – as, under Article 300(6) and (7) of the EC Treaty, international treaties ratified by the Community are binding only insofar as they are compatible with Community law (see, in particular, ¶ 308).

The Court's approach to the relations between the two legal orders recalls that of the Italian Constitutional Court in terms of the interaction between the internal legal orders of Member States and that established by the European Convention on Human Rights. The "superior" law imposes itself on the "inferior" primary law, but only within the limits set by the Constitution of the "inferior" legal order. This means that the "inferior" legal order retains the possibility to control the manner of its integration into the "superior" one, without unconditionally opening the door to the latter. In this sense, this approach can be distinguished from that adopted by many European constitutional courts to the issue of relations with the Community legal order, since the latter courts retain only fundamental principles as "counter-limits." This is confirmed by Paragraphs 282 and 285 of the *Kadi* judgment (and also by ¶¶ 301-304 if we consider the fact that the Community does not have its own Constitution and, instead, certain principles contained in the provisions of the different governing treaties perform a constitutional function).

X. THE *LOEWEN* CASE BEFORE AN INTERNATIONAL CENTRE FOR SETTLEMENT OF INVESTMENT DISPUTES ARBITRAL TRIBUNAL: THE PRINCIPLE OF SUBSIDIARITY

In the *Loewen* case, a dispute at the national level was brought first before a national judge, then before a global judge (an ICSID Arbitral Tribunal), on the basis of provisions of a supranational legal order (the NAFTA).[135] The provisions invoked in the proceeding before the ICSID Arbitral Tribunal were Articles 1102, 1105, and

---

[135] For an analysis of this case, *see* Henry Paul Monaghan, *Article III and Supranational Judicial Review*, 107 COLUM. L. REV. 833 (2007).

1110 of the NAFTA,[136] contained in Part V of the Agreement, concerning the regulation of investments. These articles establish in this field a most-favored nation principle, a principle of non-discrimination, and a principle of transparency.[137]

The *Loewen* decision involved a dispute that arose between a Canadian funeral home and funeral insurance business, part of a broader group of corporations which also included a US company (the "Loewen Group" and "Loewen Group International, Inc."), and a competitor company from Mississippi (O'Keefe), following the acquisition by the Loewen Group of a series of funeral businesses in the USA, amongst which was one owned by a Mr. Riemann in Mississippi. O'Keefe incurred losses as a result of the competition of the new industrial Group, and brought a claim for damages against Loewen before the Mississippi State Court. That

---

[136] The North American Free Trade Agreement is an agreement signed in 1992 between the United States, Canada and Mexico. It entered into force in 2004. It is a free trade treaty, modeled on the previous free trade agreement (FTA) between the US and Canada, which in turn was inspired by the European Community model. There are also two other agreements connected to NAFTA, relating to environmental cooperation (NAAEC) and labor cooperation (NAALC).

NAFTA has two principal organs: the Secretariat and the Commission. The Secretariat is divided into three sections, based in Ottowa, Mexico City and Washington DC, managed by a Secretary appointed by each Government. These organs provide administrative assistance to the Commission, which is the central, decision-making institution in NAFTA, and is composed of the Ministers responsible for international trade in each State.

[137] More precisely, Articles 1102(1) and (2) establish that "[e]ach Party shall accord to investors of another Party treatment no less favourable than that it accords, in like circumstances, to its own investors with respect to the establishment, acquisition, expansion, management, conduct, operation, and sale or other disposition of investments. 2. Each Party shall accord to investments of investors of another Party treatment no less favourable than that it accords, in like circumstances, to investments of its own investors with respect to the establishment, acquisition, expansion, management, conduct, operation, and sale or other disposition of investments." Article 1105(1) provides that "[e]ach Party shall accord to investments of investors of another Party treatment in accordance with international law, including fair and equitable treatment and full protection and security." Lastly, Article 1100 regulates expropriation and indemnity.

court, presided over by an African-American judge and consisting of a twelve-member jury, of whom eight were African-American, found for O'Keefe, awarding compensation for the losses, as well as punitive damages,[138] and providing explicitly discriminatory reasons for the decision.

Mississippi law allows for appeals only after an "appeal bond" has been paid, fixed by the Court in this instance at $625 million, to be posted within a week. Failure to do so would mean that the judgment would be executed immediately.

The extremely high level of the bond effectively precluded the Loewen Group from challenging the judgment; thus, considering themselves to have been discriminated against and treated in a manner less favorable than local businesses in the course of the Court proceedings, they brought a complaint before an Arbitral Tribunal under the relevant provisions of the NAFTA, constituted under the auspices of the ICSID.[139]

The Tribunal rejected the application in a decision of the 26th of June 2003. It recognized that the Mississippi State Court had conducted an unjust trial, in violation of NAFTA Article 1005. However, it also observed that, in order to benefit from the judicial protection afforded by NAFTA, the applicant must have exhausted local remedies (the "local remedies rule"), meaning that a State cannot be held responsible for errors made by its courts unless the matter has been ruled on by a court of final instance.[140]

---

[138] The total figure was around $500 million.

[139] The NAFTA provisions relating to the constitution of arbitral tribunals are contained in Articles 1116, 1117, 1121, and 1131 (the last of which concerns the law applicable by the tribunal).

[140] See Article 1101 of NAFTA, which establishes that "[t]his Chapter applies to measures adopted or maintained by a Party relating to: (a) investors of another Party; (b) investments of investors of another Party in the territory of the Party; and (c) with respect

The conduct of the national trial by the trial judge was – according to the Arbitral Tribunal – "a miscarriage of justice amounting to a manifest injustice as that expression is understood in international law" (¶ 54). The Loewen Group had been subjected to unjust and discriminatory treatment (¶ 119).[141] The decision of the jury had been influenced by racial prejudice (and by "local favouritism") (¶ 136). The process and the final verdict were "improper and discreditable," failing to respect "minimum standards of international law and fair and equitable treatment" (¶ 137). The "international right to a fair hearing" had been violated by the Mississippi State Court (¶ 142).

The Tribunal recognized, however, that the decision of the Mississippi Court did not constitute a final judgment: "judicial action is a single action from beginning to end so that the State has not spoken until all appeals have been exhausted" (¶ 143). And it observed that, were it to hand down a decision on issues on which internal remedies had not been exhausted, then this could lead to a conflict between the decisions of the global and national bodies. The Tribunal thus inquired whether the Loewen Group could have appealed to the Mississippi Supreme Court, in order to establish whether the verdict of the Mississippi State Court constituted "a

---

to Articles 1106 and 1114, all investments in the territory of the Party. 2. A Party has the right to perform exclusively the economic activities set out in Annex III and to refuse to permit the establishment of investment in such activities. 3. This Chapter does not apply to measures adopted or maintained by a Party to the extent that they are covered by Chapter Fourteen (Financial Services). 4. Nothing in this Chapter shall be construed to prevent a Party from providing a service or performing a function such as law enforcement, correctional services, income security or insurance, social security or insurance, social welfare, public education, public training, health, and child care, in a manner that is not inconsistent with this Chapter."

[141] In paragraph 119, the Tribunal observed that "by any standard of measurement, the trial involving O'Keefe and Loewen was a disgrace. By any standard of review, the tactics of O'Keefe's lawyers, particularly Mr Gary, were impermissible. By any standard of evaluation, the trial judge failed to afford Loewen the process that was due."

measure 'adopted or maintained' by Respondent amounting to a violation of Art. 1105" (¶ 207). Ultimately, the Tribunal held in this regard that "Loewen failed to pursue its domestic remedies, notably the Supreme Court option and that, in consequence, Loewen has not shown a violation of customary international law and a violation of NAFTA for which Respondent is responsible" (¶ 217), as the claimant had not demonstrated that it had no adequate remedy on the basis of internal law (¶ 2).[142] The global judges, therefore, were able to intervene only if all legal remedies had been exhausted at the national level.

In this decision, as in that in the *Mox Plant* case, reference was made to the notion of "comity" (¶ 230 and ¶ 233),[143] even if here only in respect of a marginal issue, namely the "requirement of continuous nationality."[144]

---

[142] Paragraph Two contains the finding of the Tribunal, and holds that "the conclusion rests on the Claimants' failure to show that Loewen had no reasonably available and adequate remedy under United States municipal law in respect of the matters of which it complains, being matters alleged to be violations of NAFTA."

[143] "Comity" is an international legal principle of uncertain definition. It has been variously described as the basis of international law; a rule of international law; a synonym for private international law; a choice-of-law rule; a principle of courtesy; a principle of good manners; a principle of convenience or of goodwill between sovereign governments; a moral necessity; a remedy or an expedient, etc. *See* Robert B. Ahdieh, *Between Dialogue and Decree: International Review of National Courts*, 79 N.Y.U. L. Rev. 2029, 2050, n. 89 (2004). The entry for "comity" in the Encyclopedia of Public International Law, however, asserts that "in public international law the notion of comity (*comitas gentium, courtoisie internationale, Völkercourtoisie*) embraces those acts, practices and rules of goodwill, amity and courteous treatment habitually observed by States in their mutual intercourse without the conviction that any legal obligation is involved;" and adds that "since a rule of comity does not involve a legal obligation, its non-observance produces no legal consequences." Two points are clear: "comity" concerns the relations between courts, and not those between legal orders more generally; and it is an "umbrella term," in the sense that it has a plurality of meanings, drawn from rules relating to the precedence or respect afforded by one judge to another.

[144] During the process the Loewen Group was incorporated into the Loewen Group International inc., assuming US and losing Canadian nationality. This could have decreased

The *Loewen* decision concerned the relationship between a supranational and a national legal order. The former prohibits discrimination against foreign investors, which had been present in the case before the NAFTA judges, who were called upon to regulate the relations between the two orders (in the absence, however, of specific rules on how to do so). They were thus forced to identify a rule regulating the relationship between the legal orders, and they found it in the principle of subsidiarity: the global judge intervenes only when all legal remedies at the national level have been exhausted, meaning that he thus carries out a superior or appeal function. This principle can also be subsumed within that of "comity," on condition that the content of the latter is precisely defined. In other words, it is not in "comity" itself that I am interested here; rather, it is in certain content that might be given to that notion, and the manner in which it is applied.

---

the "coverage" of NAFTA, and the jurisdiction of the Arbitral Tribunal, on the grounds of a violation of the "continuous nationality" requirement, which itself is "grounded in comity" (¶ 230).

CHAPTER V

"THE LEAST DANGEROUS BRANCH"

INDEX

I. THE JUDGE-MADE RULES ON THE RELATIONS BETWEEN LEGAL ORDERS

I N this paper, I have examined four sets of relations: those between national and the Community legal orders; those between national and the Council of Europe legal orders; those between the Community and different global legal orders; and those between national and supranational legal orders more generally.

None of these relations is regulated from "on high," by a more extensive legal order; indeed, regulating norms of this sort either do not exist or are very general and vague. This void is therefore filled by judges.

In each of these cases, we have seen judges at work in each of the legal orders in need of coordination, engaged in bidirectional relations and coupled together in a reciprocal endeavor (although this reciprocity does not always materialize in practice): the European Court of Justice and the Spanish and Polish Constitutional Courts in the first group of cases; the European Court of Human Rights and the Italian Constitutional Court in the second; the European Court of Human Rights and the European Court of Justice in the third; the UNCLOS Arbitral Tribunal and the European Court of Justice in the fourth; the NAFTA Arbitral Tribunal and the Mississippi State Court in the fifth; and, in the sixth and final case, the European Court of Justice – without, however, a corresponding judge from the UN legal order (which highlights usefully some of the flaws of the latter).

The proceeding analysis shows that, in the presence of a wide variety of global, supranational and State norms, which are not structured in a hierarchical manner and which leave a certain degree of freedom as to the choice of law, judges not only guarantee the juridical unity of their own orders internally, but simultaneously determine the links between the order to which they belong and external orders, regulating the relations between the different systems.

Judicial activity does not take place in a normative vacuum; quite to the contrary, it is based upon norms. These norms, however, belong to different legal orders and are also different in scope. In some cases, as noted above, the norms establish the prevalence of one legal order over another (for example, the European order over national orders, or the UN order over the European one). In other cases, they are limited to the establishment of a preference for one regulatory mechanism over another (such as, for example, the preference established by the UNCLOS for a judicial or quasi-judicial solution over other forms of conflict resolution). Lastly, there are cases in which the norms in question are limited to the institution of a judicial body, without laying down rules relating to the interaction between different legal orders. In these cases, it is judges who must establish an "order between legal orders."

These judges operate in a number of different ways. Firstly, they can "import" the external order into the internal one (the doctrines of direct effect and of primacy). In this case, an external order, despite not being in a hierarchically superior position and not compelling the abrogation of the inferior norms in cases of conflict, nevertheless renders the latter inapplicable on the basis of the distinction between spheres of competence.

Secondly, judges can integrate the internal order within the external one (the doctrines of "counter-limits" and of "interposed rules"). In the case of "counter-limits," a "superior" or external legal order is accepted by an "inferior" or internal one on the condition that the former respects the fundamental principles of the latter. In the case of "interposed rules," on the other hand, a "superior" or external law is imposed upon the primary legislation of the "inferior" or internal order, but not upon its constitutional law at all.

Thirdly, judges can establish a sphere of autonomy for the internal order with respect to the external one (the "margin of appreciation" doctrine). In this case, a "superior" or external order leaves a discretionary margin to the "inferior" or internal one.

Fourthly, judges can recognize the validity of a legal order on the condition that it provides guarantees for the protection of fundamental rights that are "equivalent" to those of another legal order.

Fifthly, judges apply the principles of "division of functions" or of "subsidiarity," recognizing the competence of the order that has been principally entrusted with the task of carrying out a particular function, or that of the order closest to the interests involved in any given controversy.

Lastly, judges introduce "junctions," "rules of engagement" or "rules of recognition" between different legal orders, which must display mutual respect (the idea of "judicial comity").

II. THE CONTEXT: FRAGMENTATION

In order to draw together the different threads of this analysis, we must consider four different aspects: the context in which the activity of judges is situated; the subjects involved (*i.e.*, the judges themselves); the activities that they carry out (and the rules on the basis of which they do so); and the problems to which all of these aspects of the judge-made global legal system give rise.

As has been noted many times, the legal context in which national, supranational and global courts operate is characterized by a plurality of legal orders that are not ordered within a system, and are thus, in principle, separated from each other (so-called "fragmentation").

There is no unity within the global space, either in that there are one hundred and ninety-two different States or in that there are around two thousand different regulatory regimes currently in existence (the latter relating to governance of the sea, the environment, agriculture, foodstuffs, work, etc.).[145]

There exists a direct correlation between fragmentation and the development of global administrative law. Fragmentation is the result of a weak constitutional framework (*e.g.*, the lack of a parliament or an executive at the global level), in turn the result of the dominant role played by States in the global space. And yet fragmentation itself has been important in the development of a body of global administrative law norms: these would not have been able to develop in a general, systematic fashion, as they would have met with considerable resistance from States and their administrations.

In order to overcome fragmentation, different governance regimes have developed a range of diverse techniques, such as creating networks of common regulatory bodies, referring to the norms of other legal orders, establishing common principles, substituting multilateralism for bilateralism, and developing other modes of

[145] On the issue of fragmentation, *see* the recent paper by Euan MacDonald & Eran Shamir-Borer, *Meeting the Challenges of Global Governance: Administrative and Constitutional Approaches*, draft for NYU Hauser Colloquium (1st October 2008).

interaction. Even this, however, is insufficient: there remains a need to move from a plurality to a system of different legal orders. And it is at this point that judges intervene, building "bridges" that link together national, supranational, and global legal orders.[146]

III. JUDGES AS THE BUILDERS OF THE GLOBAL SYSTEM OF LEGAL ORDERS

Many authors have sought to discover the reasons for which judges are being asked to carry out an ever-more extensive range of functions. Jürgen Habermas has observed that courts "speak" and "listen" as equals, and are at once authors and addressees of norms. In particular, he argues that judges interact with each other on the basis of the discursive method and the proceduralist paradigm. The democratic State, indeed, can be defined as that institutionalization of procedure and of communicative presuppositions that enables discursive opinion- and will-formation; and, according to the "discourse principle," "[o]nly those norms of action are valid to which all affected persons could assent as participants in rational discourses."[147]

---

[146] There exist, in particular, two contrasting schools of thought on the relationship between fragmentation and the role of courts. According to the first, the activity of courts at the global level is a means of tempering and overcoming fragmentation; see TREVES, *supra* note 8, at 59-67; ANNE-MARIE SLAUGHTER, A NEW WORLD ORDER 65-103 (2004); MIREILEE DELMAS-MARTY, LE RELATIF ET L'UNIVERSEL. LES FORCES IMAGINANTES DU DROIT 196 ff. (2004). The second, however, is strongly critical of this first position, maintaining that the activity of courts itself contributes to fragmentation, highlighting the risk of a "tyranny" or a "government" of judges; see Oda, *supra* note 7, at 863-872; IL GIUDICE SOVRANO. COERCING VIRTUE 163 ff. (Robert H. Bork ed., 2006); ALLARD & GARAPON, *supra* note 77, at 39 ff.; I DIRITTI IN AZIONE. UNIVERSALITÀ E PLURALISMO DEI DIRITTI FONDAMENTALI NELLE CORTI EUROPEE 57-66 (Marta Cartabia ed., 2007).

[147] *See generally*, JÜRGEN HABERMAS, BETWEEN FACTS AND NORMS: CONTRIBUTIONS TO A DISCOURSE THEORY OF LAW AND DEMOCRACY 132-151, 459 (William Rehg trans., 1996); considerations such as these can also be found in the work of the English philosopher and political scientist MICHAEL OAKESHOTT, THE VOICE OF POETRY IN THE CONVERSATION

Applying these principles to judicial activity in the global arena, we can say that each court recognizes the others because all respect the same rules (such as, for example, the principle of limitation to the particular case before them, the right to an adversarial proceeding, the obligation to provide reasoned decisions, etc.).

With specific reference to the global arena, Robert B. Ahdieh[148] has observed that "judicial dialogue" displays three characteristics. It is "ordinarily prospective rather than retrospective;" it is "bidirectional;" and it is "characterized by some dimension of voluntariness."

Jenny S. Martinez,[149] in her examination of "court-made doctrines," has observed that the European Court of Human Rights "converses rather than commands; national governments become both the authors and the addressees of the law;" and, on the basis of comments made by then-President of the European Court of Human Rights Luzius Wildhaber, she has emphasized that the fact that the Court does not possess the direct power to execute its own decisions represents an advantage: the lack of judicial "self-sufficiency" in this sense means that the States are more willing to accept the role played by courts.[150]

Lastly, Maria Rosaria Ferrarese has explained the primacy of judicial mechanisms in the regulation of the relations between legal orders by the fact that judge-made law is 'lighter' than that made by legislatures; it is capable of modifying itself.[151] Therefore, with

---

OF MANKIND (1959), republished *in* RATIONALISM IN POLITICS AND OTHER ESSAYS (1962) (pp. 196-198, dealing with "conversation").

[148] Ahdieh, *supra* note 143, at 2051-2052.

[149] Martinez, *supra* note 78, in particular at 467.

[150] On Strasbourg's accommodation strategies, *see* Nico Krisch, *The Open Architecture of European Human Rights Law*, 71 MOD. L. REV. 183, 206 ff. (2008).

[151] MARIA ROSARIA FERRARESE, IL DIRITTO AL PRESENTE. GLOBALIZZAZIONE E TEMPO DELLE ISTITUZIONI 201 (2002).

globalization, judges must sort through a stream of legal traffic that becomes denser, more intricate and more complex every day.[152] Lastly, courts tend to create a freestanding system, moving in the process beyond national confines to a degree and establishing their own interactive network that branches out along new spatial pathways.[153] These studies highlight the fact that judges can be interlocutors, and can adapt to each other reciprocally; there is no need to recognize a hierarchy between different jurisdictions. However, they fail to place sufficient emphasis on certain other structural elements that acquire particular importance in the global arena.

First of all, it should be borne in mind that the term "court" refers to not one but many different entities. When we refer to them in the study of the global legal space, we must refrain from making references to national law and culture (which are, in turn, very different from each other; it is enough to recall the difference between an Italian and a British judge). In the global context, there are permanent courts and "ad hoc" committees; permanent members of judicial bodies, and members nominated to deal with a certain question; full and genuine courts and quasi-judicial bodies. Of course, the judges involved come from diverse nations and cultures; and yet there are a number of common elements. Judges do not form a single epistemic community, but rather what we might call a single "behavioral grouping." Lastly, as has already been noted, the role of national judges (and constitutional judges in particular) in the determination of relations is not a minor one.[154]

---

[152] *Id.* at 202.

[153] *Id.* at 230. *See also* ALFONSO CATANIA, METAMORFOSI DEL DIRITTO. DECISIONE E NORMA NELL'ETÀ GLOBALE 134 (2008); DAVID ORDÓÑEZ SOLÍS, EL COSMOPOLITISMO JUDICIAL EN UNA SOCIEDAD GLOBAL. GLOBALIZACIÓN, DERECHO Y JUECES (2008).

[154] *See generally,* Eyal Benvenisti, *Reclaiming Democracy: The Strategic Uses of Foreign and International Law by National Courts*, 102 AM. J. INT'L L. 241 (2008); Philip Sales & Joanne Clement, *International Law in Domestic Courts: The Developing Framework*, 124 LAW QUARTERLY REVIEW 388 (2008).

Secondly, judges always decide on a "case-by-case" basis. Theirs is always an interstitial intervention, due to the fact that they must decide in relation to the complaint before them. No national legal order would accept the intrusion of courts if it were not recognized that it is limited to the requests of the parties to the case, and therefore necessarily concrete – and not abstract and general – in character. And the same can be said for each sectoral global regulatory system with respect to the others. The intervention of courts, however, has the same set of advantages as does the "fire alarm" system over that of "police patrol:"[155] it is more economic, because courts intervene when the need to do so presents itself; and it is more diffuse, because it is activated at the request of the interested parties.

The third characteristic of this judicial activity is its incremental nature. Courts decide on the basis of precedents, thus on fixed rails, proceeding gradually; they decide, therefore, with a high degree of predictability, but also with the possibility for making successive adjustments. Even this mode of operation facilitates the activity of judges (national, supranational, and global) as the craftsmen of the (general) global legal edifice.

In the initial phase, due to the novelty of the particular function that I have examined in this paper, there were no specific precedents and courts were thus compelled to refer to those of other judges or to start down this path without the support of precedent. But this vacuum has rapidly been filled. The incremental nature of judicial action has served to reassure States, concerned for the erosion of their sovereignty, and global regulatory regimes, concerned for the efficiency of their sectoral action.

---

[155] This is a reference to the famous distinction drawn in Mathew D. McCubbin & Thomas Schwartz, *Congressional Oversight Overlooked: Police Patrols versus Fire Alarms*, 28 AMERICAN JOURNAL OF POLITICAL SCIENCE 165 (1984).

Fourthly, judges have a characteristic "modus operandi," in that they follow common rules: they must listen to the parties before deciding (even ensuring, at times, a full and genuine adversarial hearing); they must decide on the basis of information acquired in the course of the hearing and known to the parties; and they must provide reasons for their judgment.

The fifth characteristic is that courts have a great deal of flexibility in reaching a decision, because they can alternate between activism and "deference," law-creation and self-restraint, dynamism and tolerance, rigidity and flexibility. In particular, as noted above,[156] they have frequent recourse to the principle of proportionality, and of the appropriateness of means to ends. Other actors (States, international organizations, or the organs of either) remain free to determine the ends and choose the means, while the courts evaluate the relation between them. This form of decentralization means that judges do not monopolize the connective function between legal orders, thereby establishing a division of labor between courts and State executives (along with global international organizations).

In the sixth place, courts operate – as mentioned previously – on relatively minor cases. It is true that they establish "constitutional" principles intended to govern the relations between the various different legal orders; in doing so, however, they start from questions of "low politics." This establishes a kind of division of functions between national governments, which retain control over major questions, and courts, to which are entrusted minor questions. Courts, however, take advantage of this "delegation," creating secondary circuits through the expansion of their network and the reconstruction of the "system." In this way, courts extend

---

[156] *See also* Alec Stone Sweet & Jud Mathews, *Proportionality, Balancing and Global Constitutionalism*, 47 COLUM. J. TRANSNAT'L L. 72 (2008).

the application of the "rule of law," starting from the principle of legality. In doing so, they are on the one hand acting strategically, increasing "compliance" with global norms, while on the other they are maximizing their own power, creating the conditions for further expansion. It is, thus, a self-perpetuating circle, one factor in the acceleration of the process of globalization, which contributes in a concrete manner to "de-fragmentation" insofar as it brings together orders that were created separate.

In progressing in this manner, global law corresponds to the development of national administrative law, and can be differentiated from that of national constitutional law. The former was first affirmed in areas generally considered to be of minor importance, and then extended into properly "political" areas. We can think here of the initial exclusion of "*les actes de gouvernement*" and of "*atti politici*" from the supervision of administrative judges, in France and Italy respectively, and of the respect shown by North American judges for the Presidential prerogative in matters of foreign policy and defense. National systems of constitutional law, on the other hand, have witnessed a "judicial empowerment through constitutionalization," which has come about through a "transfer of... big questions from the political sphere to the courts."[157]

Lastly, the decisions of courts demand executive action, and do not close the door to subsequent "legislative" interventions. As such, they are not definitive in character; they can be reversed by the executive or by the legislature.[158] This is a source of both weakness and strength for courts in the global arena, as States have not been

---

[157] RAN HIRSCHL, TOWARDS JURISTOCRACY. THE ORIGINS AND CONSEQUENCES OF THE NEW CONSTITUTIONALISM 213 (2004).

[158] It is worth recalling here the words of Alexander Hamilton: "the judiciary is beyond comparison the weakest of the three departments of power... it can never attack with success either of the other two." *See* THE FEDERALIST NO. 78, *supra* note 75.

entirely deprived of their sovereignty (even if it can be argued that "limited sovereignty" no longer corresponds to the typical characteristics of sovereignty itself).

These, then, are the reasons behind the success of courts in becoming an important factor in the search for cohesion between legal orders in the global arena; and they explain why courts are now so often substituted for the traditional relations of diplomatic negotiations between governments, and carry out a "constituent" function.[159]

It has been observed that "perhaps the most significant political outcome of the vision of international law as a legal system is the empowerment of courts to develop international law beyond the intention of governments."[160] The configuration of the relations between national and global legal orders, and therefore the conception of global law as a legal system, is essentially judge-made.

---

[159] One further observation: certain characteristics typical of judicial action, when carried to the global arena, manifest themselves differently, reinforcing this judicial weaving of the fabric of global law. These, however, draw attention to another important issue, which would require a further study of its own: judges, in carrying out the function indicated above, ultimately play a different role than do courts operating in the purely national arena. The latter bodies act as limits on the other branches of public power. In the global arena, however, these other branches do not exist, and courts operate instead as organs whose role is to complete the legal order.

I will not consider here the "reactions" of different legal orders, such as, for example, the reaction of national judges to the expansion of global law. On this latter point, *see* Benvenisti, *supra* note 154.

[160] Eyal Benvenisti, *The Conception of International Law as a Legal System*, 50 GERMAN YEARBOOK OF INTERNATIONAL LAW 393 (2008).

IV. A NEW "INDIRECT RULE?"

The most significant characteristic of courts in their "dialogue" in the global arena is, however, the manner in which they construct rules concerning the relations between legal orders.

The function that I have highlighted here consists in the establishment of "rules of recognition," in the sense given to that term by H.L.A. Hart: the norms whose existence is necessary for the rise of ordinary law, and from which that law derives its validity[161] (for our purposes here, rules of cohabitation between different legal orders).[162]

What do the different cases examined here have in common? Firstly, courts do not leave empty spaces: rather, they fill them in, establishing ties between different orders, as in the *Kadi* case before the European Court of Justice, in which it was affirmed that the European order is not independent from that of the United Nations (¶ 208).

Secondly, courts recognize the primacy of "superior" law, due either to the size of its sphere of validity or to the specialization of

---

[161] H.L.A. HART, THE CONCEPT OF LAW 94 ff. (2d ed. 1994). With reference to national legal orders, Hart observed that the "rule of recognition" "introduces, although in embryonic form, the idea of a legal system: for the rules are now not just a discrete unconnected set but are, in a simple way, unified." For an interesting application of the notion of a secondary rule of recognition to global law, *see* Gianluigi Palombella, *The Rule of Law Beyond the State: Failures, Promises and Theory*, 7 Int'l J. Const. L. 442 (2009).

[162] In a similar sense, it has been observed that the action of courts represents "a shift from rules of conflict to rules of engagement. These rules of engagement characteristically take the forms of a duty to engage, the duty to take into account as a consideration of some weight, or presumption of some sort." *See* Mattias Kumm, *Democratic Constitutionalism Encounters International Law: Terms of Engagement, in* THE MIGRATION OF CONSTITUTIONAL IDEAS 256, 292 (Sujit Choudhry ed., 2006).

the body charged with the exercise of a particular function.[163]   In doing so, however, they recognize the principle of "indirect rule," in which "local" norms and structures are recognized and incorporated in "superior" ones.

It is interesting to note that a principle typical of British colonialism, developed in particular between the 19th and 20th centuries by Frederick Lugard on the basis of his experiences as High Commissioner of the Protectorate of Northern Nigeria, is now being applied so many years later, and in so many different fields. This principle contained *in nuce* the rules of a dual system that enabled the emirs in their various caliphates to coexist, subordinate to the British officials operating in the district, thus transforming the emirs into agents of the British authority. This enabled the British to govern vast spaces with a relatively limited number of civil servants, whose orders were mediated through the emirs before reaching the local population. Global law affirms itself in relation to national law in precisely the same manner.[164]

---

[163] Also on the basis of Article 103 of the UN Charter, which provides that all other international agreements are subordinate to the Charter.

[164] On "indirect rule," *see* FREDERICK LUGARD, THE DUAL MANDATE IN BRITISH TROPICAL AFRICA (1922). It sets out the principal elements of the idea of "dual administration," which consisted in "native rule under the guidance and control of the British staff" (p. 228); "self-government," applied in different ways (p. 193), decentralization (pp. 96 ff), cooperation (p. 95), supervisory, management and coordination functions, as well as the collection of the taxes owed to the British colonial administration (p. 95); none of which, however, had any standardized form. See also pp. 182 ff. and 228 for a comparison with the French colonial system. The first theoretical work, which took an anthropological perspective, on "indirect rule" was that by BRONISLAW MALINOWSKI, *Indirect rule and its scientific planning*, *in* THE DYNAMICS OF CULTURE CHANGE: AN INQUIRY INTO RACE RELATIONS IN AFRICA 138 (1961).

V. THE LEGITIMACY OF THE JUDICIAL CONSTRUCTION OF THE GLOBAL LEGAL SYSTEM

The judicial construction of a global legal system creates, however, a problem: that of the legitimation of this form of judicial action.

This can be formulated in the terms used by Chief Justice Roberts of the US Supreme Court in his dissenting opinion in the famous judgment on Guantanamo Bay.[165] The Chief Justice, criticizing the majority view of the Court, observed that there were no winners from that judgment: not the prisoners in Guantanamo Bay, not the principle of *habeas corpus*, not the rule of law, and not the American people, "who today lose a bit more control over the conduct of this Nation's foreign policy to unelected, politically unaccountable judges." In sum, what Roberts was referring to is the well-known problem of the legitimation of judges in taking decisions that are general in scope and can, as a result, put them in conflict with the parliamentary majority.

In the global arena, this "counter-majoritarian difficulty" has been a source of even greater concern than it has been in the domestic setting.[166] If, in the latter context, parliaments can remedy the

---

[165] *Boumediene v. Bush*, 128 S. Ct. 2229, 2279(2008); see in particular p. 2293. It is worth noting that, in its judgment in *Medellín v. Texas* 552 US 491 (2008), the US Supreme Court explicitly raised the question of the displacement of "sensitive foreign policy decisions" from the "political branch" to the courts.

[166] It has been observed that "in less than a decade, an unprecedented concept has emerged to submit international politics to judicial procedures. It has spread with extraordinary speed and has not been subjected to systematic debate, partly because of the intimidating passion of its advocates. To be sure, violations of human rights, war crimes, genocide, and torture have so disgraced the modern age and in such a variety of places that effort to interpose legal norms to prevent or punish such outrages does credit to its advocates. The danger is that it is being pushed to extremes which risk substituting the tyranny of judges for that of governments; historically, the dictatorship of the virtuous has often led

"legislative abdication of power" with subsequent legislative interventions, the "migration of power" towards judges in the global arena is less easily rectified, for to do so requires concerted action by States.

This concern is, however, misguided. It is based on the assumption that modern public authorities have only one component: democracy (elections – majority of voters – majority of the elected – general will). Such authorities, however, are all "mixed" regimes (albeit to different degrees), with both a democratic component and a liberal one. Both components fulfill the same function: that of keeping power under control. The democratic component does so through the periodic election of representatives to whom the holders of power are answerable. The liberal component, however, fulfills its function through the supervision of the respect by the holders of power of applicable legal principles. Therefore, although the means by which this function is performed change, the function itself does not.

The two components have different historical origins. As Pasquale Pasquino has observed, "the State based on the rule of law was theorized by Montesquieu, who showed no particular interest

to inquisitions and even witch hunts." The International Criminal Court "in its present form of assigning the ultimate dilemmas of international politics to unelected jurists – and to an international judiciary at that –... represents such a fundamental change in American constitutional practice that a full national debate and full participation of Congress are imperative. Such a momentous revolution should not come about by tacit acquiescence in the decision of the House of Lords or by dealing with the ICC issue with a strategy of improving specific clauses rather than as a fundamental issue of principle." *See* HENRY KISSINGER, DOES AMERICA NEED A FOREIGN POLICY? 273, 279 (2001). On these issues, *see also* Joseph H.H. Weiler, *The Geology of International Law – Governance, Democracy and Legitimacy*, 64 ZEITSCHRIFT FÜR AUSLÄNDISCHES ÖFFENTLICHES RECHT UND VÖLKERRECHT 547 (2004), in which the author examines the development of international law, highlighting that while conflicts between legal orders were originally resolved only by means of negotiations between national governments, this role is now increasingly entrusted to extra-State quasi-judicial bodies.

in democracy (either in its antique or modern forms), and was first put into practice in Prussia at the end of the 18th century, under the enlightened monarchy of Frederick the Great; the rights of man were formalized by a Revolution that also banned political parties."[167]

Now, if the historical roots of democracy and liberty are distinct, and these two notions are distinct components of public power, then the issue of the popular or democratic legitimation of judges is a "false problem;" the balance and restraint of public powers is achieved thanks precisely to the simultaneous presence of both components – which can also conflict.

---

[167] Pasquale Pasquino, *Lo spettro e l'esorcista* (unpublished manuscript on file with the author).

THIS paper is the product of research conducted during the last two years, the results of which were in part set out in lectures in Florence on the 27th of May 2008, and in Rome on the 25th and 29th of May, the 19th of June and the 1st of July 2008, at the *Istituto di Scienze Umane* (SUM) and the Institute for Research on Public Administration (IRPA) respectively. The Lectures were collected by Elisa D'Alterio, who also made use of my notes and preparatory materials in doing so. I have since written a subsequent version.

I would like to thank Mariangela Benedetti, Marco Pacini and Elisa D'Alterio for their research assistance with the cases, and the last of these in particular for having transcribed the oral version of the lectures and having checked the sources, as well as for subsequent research necessary to the final version.

Lorenzo Casini, Renato Finocchi and Aldo Sandulli read and commented upon a preliminary version of this paper. Lorenzo Casini, Elisa D'Alterio and Euan MacDonald also provided comments and other assistance in the final revision.

S. C.

THE PRINTING OF THIS BOOK
WAS COMPLETED ON 30 JULY
2   O   I   O

926